LOST RAIL
OF LANCASHIRE

Other Railways titles available from
Countryside Books include:

Lost Railways of Berkshire

Lost Railways of Cheshire

Lost Railways of the Chilterns

Lost Railways of Dorset

Lost Railways of East Anglia

Lost Railways of Hampshire

Lost Railways of Herefordshire & Worcestershire

Lost Railways of Kent

Lost Railways of Leicestershire & Rutland

Lost Railways of Merseyside & Greater Manchester

Lost Railways of Middlesex

Lost Railways of Northumberland

Lost Railways of Nottinghamshire

Lost Railways of Shropshire

Lost Railways of Staffordshire

Lost Railways of Surrey

Lost Railways of Sussex

Lost Railways of Wiltshire

Lost Railways of North & East Yorkshire

LOST RAILWAYS
OF LANCASHIRE

Gordon Suggitt

COUNTRYSIDE BOOKS
NEWBURY, BERKSHIRE

First published 2003
© Gordon Suggitt 2003

Reprinted, with revisions, 2004, 2007

COUNTRYSIDE BOOKS
3 Catherine Road
Newbury, Berkshire

To view our complete range of books,
please visit us at
www.countrysidebooks.co.uk

ISBN 1 85306 801 2

Designed by Graham Whiteman
Maps and photographs by the author
Cover illustration by Colin Doggett

The cover picture shows a Hughes/Fowler class 4 2-6-0 loco ('Crab')
at Brooksbottoms

Produced through MRM Associates Ltd., Reading
Typeset by Mac Style Ltd, Scarborough, N. Yorkshire
Printed by Cambridge University Press

CONTENTS

ABBREVIATIONS

The following abbreviations are used in this book:

BR	British Railways
CLC	Cheshire Lines Committee
ELR	East Lancashire Railway
FP&WRJR	Fleetwood, Preston & West Riding Junction Railway
G&KER	Garstang & Knott End Railway
KER	Knott End Railway
LMS	London, Midland & Scottish Railway
LNWR	London & North Western Railway
LS&PJR	Liverpool, Southport & Preston Junction Railway
LUR	Lancashire Union Railway
LYR	Lancashire & Yorkshire Railway
NUR	North Union Railway
P&LR	Preston & Longridge Railway
RCTS	Railway Correspondence and Travel Society
SCLER	Southport & Cheshire Lines Extension Railway
WLR	West Lancashire Railway

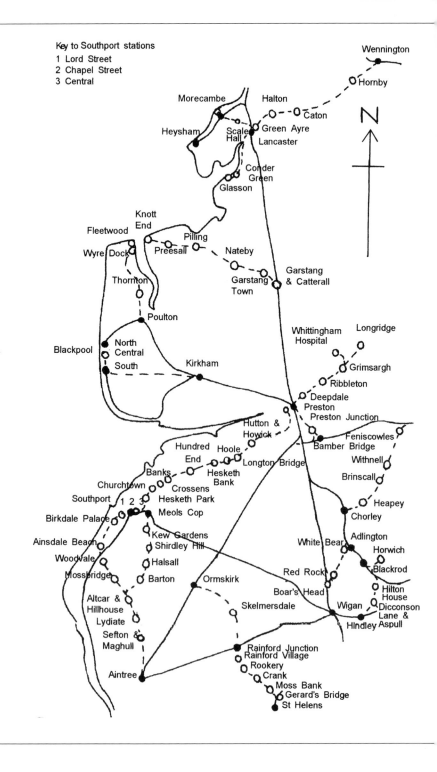

Station names are generally those in use at the Grouping of 1923

1 = Ewood Bridge/Irwell Vale 2 = Clough Fold
3 = Waterfoot 4 = Stacksteads

———— = existing railway – – – = disused railway
● = open station O = closed station

Intermediate stations on exisiting lines have usually been omitted,
also halts on closed lines - see later maps.

ACKNOWLEDGEMENTS

I would like to acknowledge the help and resources provided by the libraries of Lancashire and adjoining areas of Greater Manchester and Merseyside. I would also like to thank individually Alec Radnedge and Joe Booth for their reminiscences, Richard Casserley, Geoffrey Robinson and Keith Hick for use of their photo collections, Arthur Haynes and Mrs Shirley Peden for their help with photo copyright, and Mike Clark for his help with loco identification. Lastly I am particularly grateful to my wife Jen for her help, encouragement and careful checking of the text.

Introduction

Towering mill chimneys, cobbled streets, smoke-blackened ter-
raced houses – are these the images suggested by a book on
Lancashire's lost railways? Those seeking such scenes here will
be out of luck, as even the photographs from yesteryear show
few mill chimneys. Yes, towns of the former cotton industry fill
its southern margins, but present-day Lancashire is a surprisingly rural county. In 1974 the one-time heartland of its industrial areas was included within 'new' counties to the south –
Merseyside and Greater Manchester. Apart from a southern tier
of industrial towns, and its largely built-up coastline, most of
Lancashire is countryside, and a large part of its central-north-
ern area has never had any railways.

What 'lost railways' do we have in Lancashire? Firstly routes
to the coast account for about a quarter of the total of closures,
both those to remote locations such as Glasson and Knott End,
and also some routes to the major holiday resorts of Blackpool,
Morecambe and Southport, due to reduced demand. Secondly,
there are those lines regarded as excess to requirements within
the southern industrial zone. Some of these only gave access to
small factory towns like Barnoldswick and Bacup. Others were
more important links, such as Blackburn to Chorley and
Accrington to Bury, but still axed particularly in the Beeching
cuts of the 1960s. Lastly, there are three cross-country routes,
using the Lune and Ribble valleys and the Aire Gap, to gain
access to Yorkshire, perhaps the most surprising closures of all.

The eagle-eyed reader will have spotted the reference to
Southport, particularly in terms of post-1974 Lancashire. Yes,
despite strenuous efforts, that seaside resort is still within the
Merseyside area. A glance at the contents and general map will
show that the southern limit of Lancashire has not been strictly

adhered to. Railway lines mostly built well over a century ago did not come to an end at county boundaries, past or present. Thus all three of Southport's closed lines have stretches within present-day Lancashire before reaching that resort, and have been included here. Similarly lines from Ormskirk, Chorley, Accrington and Bacup have been covered as far as their destinations in the Merseyside and Greater Manchester areas.

In addition, three lines included here were entirely within Greater Manchester. These tidy up the coverage along the southern margins, but one has added significance. This was the line to the town of Horwich, and more importantly its locomotive works. From 1889 over 1,800 engines were built there, and over 50,000 repaired, in almost a century until closure in 1983. Its importance lay not just in numbers of locos, but in its status as the major engineeering centre for the Lancashire & Yorkshire Railway (LYR). Although other pre-Grouping companies are also represented by lines featured in this book – the Midland, the Cheshire Lines Committee and the LNWR – it was the LYR that dominated the early history of the area's railways. By the time of its amalgamation with the LNWR in 1922, the LYR solely or jointly operated 16 out of the 25 lines featured here. Thus it seems logical to include the Horwich branch as the last of the book's chapters, despite it being a mile or two outside 'Lancashire'. However, it is in the extreme north of the county, away from the former LYR's influence, that we begin this survey of the lines that used to be and what they have left behind, including three preservation schemes.

Gordon Suggitt

1
Down The Lune

Wennington Junction to Lancaster/
Lancaster (Green Ayre) to Morecambe (Promenade)/
The Glasson Dock branch

The hub of the local railways – Lancaster Castle station looking south before the rebuilding of 1902, with the line to Green Ayre at the bottom left. (Author's collection)

Wennington Junction to Lancaster

The historic city and former county town of Lancaster was first reached by rail from Preston in 1840. In 1846 a line was built north from Lancaster to Carlisle. The same year, the Royal Assent was given for a line along the Lune valley to be built by the North Western Railway, a group of landowners and industrialists

13

largely based in Lancaster. It is usually referred as the 'Little' North Western, to distinguish it from the mighty LNWR. Its original proposal was for a line from the Leeds & Bradford Railway at Skipton to the Lancaster & Carlisle Railway at Low Gill, with branches including one to Lancaster. The 'main line' is beyond the scope of this book, and it is the Lancaster branch that is dealt with here, at least the portion west from Wennington Junction, just within present-day Lancashire.

Construction work on the branch began in 1848, and on 31st October 1849 a train of two locomotives hauling seven carriages set off from Green Ayre station at Lancaster to a temporary station at Wennington. Intermediate stations had been built at Halton, Caton and Hornby, plus short-lived ones at Wray (closed 1850) and Claughton (closed 1853). Services in November 1849 were advertised as three trains daily each way between Poulton

Two ex-LMS mainstays of the Lancashire lines at Wennington Junction in 1959. At the left, a Black Five 4-6-0 heads a train for Carnforth while a class 4P 2-6-4T waits to back into Wennington station for the Morecambe portion. (J.A.G.H. Coltas)

A peaceful scene at Crook O'Lune showing the disused railway's five-arch viaduct, with the more famous road bridge behind. (Author)

(Morecambe) and Leeds, although a horse-bus had to be used between Wennington and the 'main line' at Clapham. The following month a single-track link was opened from Green Ayre to Lancaster's main (Castle) station, and in 1850 completion of the line east of Wennington allowed a daily service of five trains each way from Lancaster to Leeds. That year the line east of Hornby was doubled, although it was not until 1889 that this was done for the section between Hornby and Lancaster.

The 'Little' North Western was not a financial success and its board was forced to look elsewhere for support. Its preferred option was to lease the company in 1859 to the Midland Railway (which had worked the line for the previous seven years), although the full takeover did not take place until 1871. By 1911 the Midland was running twelve trains each way daily from Lancaster (and Morecambe) to West Yorkshire, including

15

Halton station and its goods shed were rebuilt after a fire in 1907 and are now used by Lancaster University for its rowing club. (Author)

residential expresses with Club carriages (see Chapter 3). The same number ran for the LMS in the summer of 1938, two of them boat trains for Belfast and the Isle of Man. Even after 1945 there were still eight through trains daily on this route, plus many summer excursions to Morecambe.

However, six trains daily were using the alternative route via Carnforth to Wennington (the Furness & Midland Joint line of 1862), and it was this line that was suggested for retention in the Beeching Report of 1963. The line between Wennington and Green Ayre was among those listed for closure; Hornby station had already shut in 1957 and Caton in 1961. Thus, on 1st January 1966, the line saw its last passenger services, although at this time there were still a dozen freight trains a day. These only lasted another 18 months, when the line closed altogether, except for the curve from Lancaster Castle through Green Ayre

British Railways was unlikely to have solved its financial problems with the receipts from this toll bridge over the Lune, linking Halton village with its station, judging by these charges in 1965. (F.W. Shuttleworth)

to Lancaster power station, which remained in use for coal trains up to 1976.

This route has survived better than most 'lost' railways. Both the curve from Lancaster Castle station to Green Ayre and the next five miles up the Lune valley have been retained as a footpath/cycleway. The station building at Halton is still in use, while nearby the bridge over the Lune was constructed from parts of the 1864 railway bridge at Lancaster when this was replaced by the Greyhound Bridge. Caton's station building has gone, but the stationmaster's house and goods shed (now used as a church!) remain. Soon after Caton, the usable section ends at Bull Beck by the A683. From here on, the line to Wennington Junction has mostly returned to farmland, and Hornby station has been demolished.

Lancaster (Green Ayre) to Morecambe (Promenade)

Although often regarded as the seaward end of the route along the Lune valley, this line was proposed in a separate scheme, and was built first, operating its own often distinctive services as well as through trains from the coast to West Yorkshire. The scheme was put forward by the Morecambe Harbour & Railway Company in 1846 for a line to link St George's Quay, Lancaster to the coast at Poulton, as the settlement of Morecambe was then known. This opened in 1848 with eleven trains on weekdays from Lancaster (Green Ayre) to Poulton, terminating at a wooden shed on the harbour's jetty. Services were operated by the 'Little' North Western which by then had taken over the original company.

Over the next couple of years Green Ayre station was linked to Lancaster's main (Castle) station, rail services were extended into Yorkshire, and ferry sailings were introduced, first to Piel Pier (for Barrow) then to Northern Ireland. A new passenger station for Poulton opened at Northumberland Street, and a stone quay with a more permanent station was built at the harbour.

The site of Green Ayre station is now a park, although the goods yard crane from Hornby station acts as a reminder of its past. In the background is the Greyhound Bridge, formerly used by the railway to Morecambe Promenade station. (Author)

However, problems with the tides meant that in 1867 most ferry services were switched to Piel Pier, later to Barrow, and did not return to the south shore of Morecambe Bay until the completion of Heysham Harbour in 1904. The 'Stone Jetty' station was relegated to goods duties, and from 1904 to 1933 the jetty was used for ship-breaking, most notably the White Star liner *Majestic* in 1914.

To return to the railway, the line (now operated by the Midland) was extended to Heysham in 1904, and a Lancaster-Morecambe-Heysham service using the Midland's only steam railmotors was introduced. In 1907 Northumberland Street was replaced by the new Promenade station, right on the sea front, and the following year electric trains took over the local service. These used alternating current at 6,600 volts supplied by

19

Horwich-built Black Five no 44949 waits at Morecambe Promenade's lengthy covered island platform in 1963, with the open platforms on the left. (G. Harrop)

overhead equipment. Easy reversing in and out of the stations at Green Ayre and Morecambe Promenade allowed as many as 29 Morecambe to Lancaster trains each weekday by 1912, crossing the new Greyhound Bridge over the Lune. Twelve of these were steam-hauled trains continuing on to Leeds and Bradford. In addition there were Midland boat trains from Heysham, such as the 'Belfast Boat Express' to Leeds, which could bypass Morecambe by using Torrisholme Junctions 1 and 2. However, trains for Heysham from the LNWR main line, including the 'Ulster Express', still had to reverse at Promenade station. This greatly added to congestion at Morecambe, especially after 1928 when the LMS concentrated its Northern Ireland services at Heysham.

Morecambe's links with West Yorkshire were emphasised by the introduction of the daily residential express to Leeds and

Bradford, complete with Club carriages – see Chapter 3. Even in the 1950s the 'resi' was still the train of the day out of Morecambe Promenade station. The holiday trade links were also still strong, particularly during Bradford's August holiday weeks (known there as 'Bowling Tide'). For example, in 1950 there was an extra Friday evening Bradford-Morecambe train, followed by six more by 10 am next morning, on both holiday weekends.

Local developments at this time included the replacement of the electric trains, which had been regarded as 'life-expired' as early as 1940. They were kept going until 1951, then replaced initially by steam haulage until refurbished ex-Metropolitan Railway electric sets were ready two years later. These had been built as early as 1914 and were described as having 'a certain period charm'. In 1957 a new though short-lived station was added at Scale Hall, and the following year services to Promenade station were increased by the closure of the former

The last day of service for the Morecambe and Heysham electric units – 1st January 1966. (Author's collection)

21

The ornate frontage of Morecambe Promenade station, built in 1907 and now in use as an arts centre. (Author)

LNWR station at Euston Road (except for summer Saturday traffic up to 1963). However, the line was doomed by the Beeching Report of 1963. On 1st January 1966 electric trains on the ex-Midland line to Morecambe ended and Scale Hall and Green Ayre stations were closed. Morecambe kept services to Lancaster, operated by diesel multiple units on the ex-LNWR tracks via Bare Lane, and to Leeds via Carnforth (regular direct trains to Bradford had ended the previous year). These services continue today but not from Promenade station. In 1994 it was replaced by a new 'bus shelter' style station nearer the town centre, close to the site of the old Northumberland Street station.

Perhaps surprisingly, the Promenade station building was not demolished but refurbished as the Platform Music and Community Arts Centre in 1997. The nearby 'Stone Jetty' and its station of 1853 had been restored and re-opened to the public

The attractively restored Stone Jetty still retains its station building of 1853–67, built in association with ferry sailings. (Author)

two years earlier. Most of the former Midland line, through the site of the short-lived Scale Hall station, is now a footpath and cycleway. This leads to the Greyhound Bridge, also still in use, though walkers and cyclists have to share it with northbound traffic out of Lancaster, following its conversion to a road bridge in 1972.

The Glasson Dock branch

Glasson Dock was opened in 1787 at the mouth of the Lune to serve as an outport for Lancaster, where access by ship was becoming difficult due to the river silting up. In 1826, the dock was linked to the Lancaster Canal by a basin and a three mile branch canal, which gave access to Kendal and Preston. In 1845, the first rail link was proposed, and there were three more

23

Glasson Dock is still in use for pleasure craft and some commercial activity.
(Author)

schemes before the LNWR leased the canal in 1864. Seven years later the LNWR put forward its own plan for a rail link, which was accepted by the port commissioners. However, it was another seven years before an Act was obtained for the railway, and 1883 before the 5½ mile branch from Lancaster finally opened.

The line left a bay platform at the north end of Lancaster Castle station and swung through 90° and down a 1 in 50 bank to reach New Quay on the Lune, with quayside sidings. Next were the imposing Lune Mills of the linoleum-manufacturer James Williamson, where 2 ft 9 inch gauge lines worked by two Dick, Kerr 0-4-0 locos led into the works. By now the line was on level ground close to the river, and was closed due to flooding in 1907 and 1927. Initially the only station was at Glasson, shortly before the canal basin, the line continuing past a five-storey brick warehouse (now demolished) to the dock. Soon

The May 1954 'North Lancashire' railtour visits Glasson, with the former station building visible in the centre and buildings by the dock at the extreme right. (Author's collection)

after the opening a second station was built at Conder Green and a private halt provided at Ashton Hall, from which the second James Williamson took his title of Lord Ashton after he became its owner in 1884. An arrangement was made whereby the train would stop there for Lord Ashton when needed. A contrast in lineside accommodation was to be found at the three crossing keepers' cottages, which were without running water, electricity or gas. At Aldcliffe, even the well's water was condemned, and the last tenants in the 1950s, who paid six shillings a week in rent, received all their water by train!

The Royal Train with King George V and Queen Mary aboard stayed overnight at Glasson Dock in 1917, but normal passenger services were never intensive, usually comprising five trains each way on weekdays, and usage declined markedly in 1928 due to competition from buses. The LMS claimed a loss on the passenger service of £1,500 in 1929 and applied for closure in

1930. Local people thought it significant that Lord Ashton died in May 1930, although the line was only one of 23 branches closed by the LMS that year. The last day of passenger operations was July 6th, when two extra trains ran from Lancaster, the last train being at 9.30 pm from Glasson.

Freight was the main reason for the line's construction and there was a daily goods train over the whole branch until the Second World War. By 1947 this was only running 'as required' and next year the first attempt was made to close the branch altogether. However, the line was still busy with daily workings to Williamson's mills and power station, and also up to 1960 to Lancaster's gasworks. In September 1964 the line was cut back to Lune Mills, which stopped using the railway in 1969, after which it was lifted. Most of the route was converted into a footpath and cycleway in the 1970s and the former line can be followed from Aldcliffe past the overgrown platform for Ashton Hall. At Conder Green, there is the crossing keeper's cottage

Another railtour to visit Glasson was hauled by ex-LMS class 4 2-6-0 no 42752. (J. Davenport)

At Conder Green, the trackbed and bridge over the River Conder are used for the Lancashire Coastal Way footpath, while the building was formerly the crossing keeper's cottage. (Author)

and the gateposts are still in their stone bases (the station site is now a car park and picnic area). Nothing is left of the railway facilities at Glasson except for the stationmaster's house, though the port still remains busy.

2
The 'Pilling Pig'

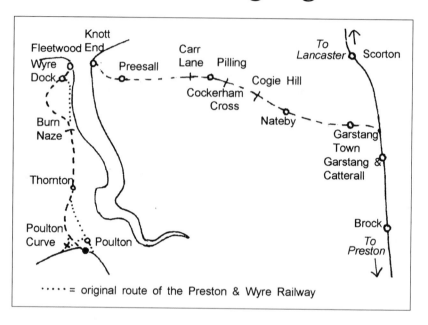

..... = original route of the Preston & Wyre Railway

The Garstang & Knott End Railway

The small market town of Garstang gained its first rail access with an inconveniently sited station (later called Garstang & Catterall) on the Lancaster & Preston Junction Railway of 1840 (the present West Coast Main Line). In 1864 an Act was passed for the Garstang & Knot-End (*sic*) Railway to link this station to the town and the tiny village of Knott End by the Wyre estuary. This was promoted by local landowners, initially with grand schemes for the new line to link to West Yorkshire and the Humber, though this was soon reduced to a local line serving an area which was once desolate peat bog but was now being reclaimed for farming.

28

Five years were allowed in the Act for construction, but financial difficulties meant that by 1867 only ½ mile of trackbed had been built, and the company appealed for an extension. In the same year, it was also decided to build the line only as far as Pilling, a distance of 7 miles, leaving the remaining 4½ miles to Knott End for some future date. Even so, construction costs came to £150,000 rather than the £60,000 estimate, and there was no money left for stock. Eventually means were found to hire a 0-4-2 tank engine *Hebe*, four carriages, twenty-four wagons and two brake vans for the opening, which took place without much ceremony on 14th December 1870 (although trains had been running since the 5th).

The initial service was nine trains each way daily (except Sundays) from Garstang & Catterall to Garstang Town, three of these continuing to Pilling via a station at Winmarleigh (called

The G&KER starting point at Garstang & Catterall, seen in 1957. Its line began on the far side of the left-hand platform and continued parallel to the main line tracks towards the distant road bridge. (H.C. Casserley)

Garstang & Catterall in 2002. Transrail class 60 no 60055 'Thomas Barnardo' passes a scene cleared of the former station apart from the station-master's house amidst the trees in the background. (Author)

Nateby from 1902) and request halts at Cogie Hill and Cockerham Cross. All the trains were mixed – passengers and freight – and all hauled by *Hebe*, which was thus in service sixteen hours a day, six days a week. Not surprisingly, little maintenance was done and by March 1872 services had to be suspended for two days while *Hebe* was overhauled, only to be repossessed for rent arrears the next month. Over the next three years a semblance of a service was kept going only by horse traction, but in 1874 the line was put into receivership. During the next year, two tank locos were leased, and first goods and then passenger services resumed. The track was relaid, stations refurbished, and even the debts paid off by 1896. There were various changes in engine, often by part-exchange, but it is *Farmer's Friend* that has gone down in history as its piercing

An earlier version of this 1938 Sentinel steam railcar handled most passenger services on the line in the last years of 'independence' before 1923. (J.A.G.H. Coltas)

The end of the line – Knott End station in September 1930, six months after closure. Visible are the stationmaster's house (centre) with to the right the water tank and signal box. (Locomotive & General Railway Photographs)

whistle earned it the nickname 'Pilling Pig', a name that stuck with the line until the final days of operation.

In 1898 a new Act was passed incorporating a separate Knott End Railway as a light railway for the remaining 4½ miles of the original route. Predictably this scheme too was soon in financial difficulties, but was saved by the development of a salt mine near Preesall, which required a 1½ mile branch from Knott End. This project allowed the completion of the KER by 1908 and its takeover of the G&KER in the same year. Stations were built at Knott End and Preesall, and a halt at Carr Lane. By 1911 there were three weekday trains each way over the full length of the line, plus a morning train from Garstang & Catterall to Garstang Town, and an evening one from Knott End to Garstang Town.

At the time of the reorganisation of 1923, the KER was the smallest constituent of the LMS with just three small tank engines,

This example at Nateby is probably the least-altered of the line's surviving crossing keepers' cottages (Author)

A new Pilling Pig? A Hudswell Clarke 0-6-0T (built in 1955) has been externally restored and put on display at the entrance to Fold House Caravan Park in Pilling. (Author)

and the larger *Blackpool*, bought for the salt trade (one of the heaviest engines ever on Britain's light railways). The LMS actually increased passenger services over the whole line to six trains each way on weekdays, but the death knell came with a dispute with the United Alkali Co over rates for haulage to and from the mine, whose trade in salt and coal totalled almost 80,000 tons in 1922. This resulted in a brine pipeline under the Wyre to the company's Burn Naze works, so that the trade was lost to the former G&KER. Without it the line was not viable, and shut for passenger services in 1930. The last passenger train returned to Knott End on March 29th, with crowds both on the train and at the level crossings to see it pass. The line remained as a goods branch, though passenger excursions continued until 1939 and the Royal Train twice stayed on the line overnight during World War II.

Goods services to Knott End lasted to 1950, and the track west of Pilling was lifted the next year. A daily goods train, still known as the 'Pilling Pig', ran to Garstang and Pilling until 1963, and to Garstang Town for another two years. However, the line closed altogether on 16th August 1965 and most of the route has now returned to farmland. A stretch of nearly a mile has been retained as a footpath near Knott End, where the station was still recognisable for many years, despite its new use as a café (it has now been extensively rebuilt). No other stations remain, though several crossing keepers' houses are still in use as residences.

3
The Fylde Coast

Fleetwood/Blackpool Central

Gateway to the Fylde – Preston station in 1963 with at the left ex-LMS Jubilee class 4-6-0 no 45703 'Thunderer' on a Blackpool relief train. (A.C. Gilbert)

Fleetwood

The Fylde is the name given to the large coastal plain between the rivers Wyre and Ribble, well away from the route of North West England's most famous early railway, the Liverpool & Manchester Railway of 1830. One of the 700 guests at that line's opening ceremony was Peter Hesketh, High Sheriff of Lancashire. During the same year he was on a committee in Preston to look into a similar railway to a port location on the Fylde coast. Various sites were examined but by 1835 one by the

35

estuary of the River Wyre had been chosen, and the Preston & Wyre Railway and Harbour Company incorporated. By that time Hesketh had become Mr (later Sir) Peter Hesketh Fleetwood, taking the latter name from his maternal forebears. In 1836, he laid the first stone of the town on the new site, Wyreton, with next to it a fashionable seaside resort to be built and called Fleetwood in his honour.

The railway from a new station at Maudlands in Preston was completed in 1840, passing through stations at Kirkham and Poulton, then over a tidal inlet before reaching Fleetwood. This meant a two-mile crossing of an 'inland sea', partly on a stone-faced embankment and partly on piles, occasionally washed right over by the waves! This must have added excitement to the opening ceremony, on 15th July 1840, when two locos, *North Star* and *Duchess*, pulled a train from Preston to Fleetwood, where 400 guests sat down to a lavish meal at the newly completed Station House.

The railway was an instant success, with 20,000 passengers carried in the first month, rather than the 15,000 expected annually. In 1842 one of the first rail excursions took place, when more than 2,000 'hymn-singing pupils and teachers' travelled for a day out from Preston. However, the opening of the first line to Blackpool in 1846 soon took away most of the trippers. The new port too was popular, by 1840 providing sailings to Bardsea for the Lake District at a charge of 2s 6d. These were followed by services to Roa Island (for Barrow), the Isle of Man, and Belfast (four trips each way per week by 1845). The service to Ardrossan was, however, short-lived – the dream of Fleetwood as a key point on a rail-sea service to Scotland (taking 27 hours for the journey between London and Glasgow) was ended by the completion of the West Coast Main Line in 1848.

By then financial problems – the line had been woefully underfunded – had forced Sir Peter and his board out. A local board had taken over and leased the line initially to the Manchester & Leeds Railway in 1846. Improvements were made including four additional halts and, more significantly, an alternative to the tidal stretch of line. At first this was just a single track following the shore but this was later doubled, leading to the abandonment of the old embankment. The lease passed jointly to the LYR and LNWR in 1849, though it was the LYR that did most to promote the port, opening the first dock in 1877 and developing the facilities to provide 2,700 ft of quay space, 8 miles of railway tracks, a 15 acre timber pond (later converted into the port's fish dock), 10 acres of wet dock and a 30,000 ton grain elevator. In 1883 the ferry port was also improved, with a new Fleetwood station giving covered access for passengers direct to the quay.

The rail route also underwent changes. New stations were added at Thornton-Cleveleys (its eventual name) in 1865, Singleton (1870), and Wyre Dock (replacing the original Fleetwood terminus in 1885). In 1896 a major improvement was carried out at Poulton. The original alignment here had resulted in a very sharp curve onto the Blackpool line. An express heading back to Stockport in 1893 took the curve too fast and

Stanier class 4P no 42643 pulls away from Fleetwood station with a stopping train for Manchester in 1956. (J.A.G.H. Coltas)

37

The Fleetwood to Blackpool service was one of those using LYR railmotors such as this example, seen as LMS no 10610 at Horwich in 1932. (J.A.G.H. Coltas)

derailed, killing the driver and two passengers. The new junction resulted in trains for Fleetwood curving back after a new Poulton station. The old station was left on a spur and relegated to goods duties, though these lasted until 1968.

A further curve at Poulton in 1899 allowed for trains between Blackpool and Fleetwood, initially 19 weekday trains each way. Nine years later a railmotor service was introduced on this line, with additional halts at Poulton Curve (until 1952) and Burn Naze. The LYR railmotor consisted of a tiny 0-4-0 tank engine originally attached to a single passenger coach, with at its far end a special compartment equipped with remote control gear. This allowed the train on its return journey to be driven from the coach, the fireman staying with the engine. The coach's seats were reversible, and there were steps that could be let down at

38

halts without platforms. The LYR's first two railmotors were built by Kerr Stuart at Stoke, then the design was modified at the company's Horwich works for a further 18 railmotors, with additional coaches to act as trailers at busy times. This was one of seven lines in this book to use railmotors, some of which stayed in service until the 1940s.

Fleetwood's heyday was probably before the First World War, with over 100,000 passengers sailing to Belfast alone in 1900. The opening of Heysham Harbour in 1904 ultimately spelt the end for Fleetwood's ferry sailings, though it was not until 1928 that the last Belfast ferry left. Regular summer sailings to the Isle of Man continued up to 1961, when they were ended due to the cost of repairs needed to the quay. Without the ferry sailings, there was little need for the station at the quay and in 1966 the rail service was cut back to the former Wyre Dock station, more conveniently sited for the town and renamed Fleetwood. The service to Blackpool had already gone, with the last train on 1st November

Another ex-LYR loco, 0-6-0 no 12155, is seen here at Fleetwood engine shed prior to its withdrawal in December 1947. (R.K. Blencowe collection)

Seen near Poulton in 1963, Fairburn class 4P no 42153 heads a Fleetwood-Preston local service of four coaches and two fish vans! (F. Dean)

Cold comfort at the bleak expanse of Fleetwood docks, with an unidentified ex-LYR Aspinall 0-8-0 engine. (Author's collection)

1964 carrying only two passengers. Next year the five daily fish trains, two of them to London, ended as the trade switched to road haulage. However, the 20 or so passenger trains each weekday to Poulton or Kirkham were thought to be safe, as the line was not due for closure by Beeching. However, it was not listed for retention in 1968, and despite hearings the next year, the last passenger train from Fleetwood ran on Saturday, 30th May 1970.

The former Preston & Wyre line remains in use for Blackpool North trains as far as Poulton, but the section north to Fleetwood has gone out of use. It had been kept for goods services to Wyre Dock power station up to its closure in 1981, and was then cut back to ICI's Hillhouse works at Burn Naze until that complex too shut in 1999. At present only rusting tracks remain north of Poulton but the route may yet be re-used as part of an ambitious scheme to extend Blackpool's tramway network.

ICI chemical trains kept the line open as far as the Hillhouse works until its closure in 1999. Here ex-War Department Austerity class 2-8-0 no 90399 passes the famous water troughs at Salwick, west of Preston, in 1964. (F. Dean)

Blackpool Central

A splendid overhead view of Blackpool Central station in the 1930s, showing the six covered platforms and eight open ones for excursion traffic. (R.S. Carpenter)

There can be few, if any, 'lost railway' sites anywhere in the country that can match the scale of Blackpool Central station and its approaches. The station buildings, 1½ miles of platform and 34 parallel sidings tracks have now all disappeared. It is difficult to comprehend the sheer volume of the holiday traffic to Blackpool in the past. On August Bank Holiday Monday 1938, for example, as many as 451 special trains were required to bring day trippers to the resort. Significantly, 6,300 buses were also used that day. Now the remaining rail traffic (though tiny by comparison) is handled by the stations at Blackpool North and Blackpool South. The Central site is ironically a car park, and its 'New Line' from Kirkham largely used for road access from the M55 motorway.

Blackpool's first rail route was a branch from the Preston & Wyre Railway at Poulton, opened in 1846, to the present-day Blackpool North station. The precursor of Central station

Austerity class no 90227 takes the 'New Line' near Kirkham with an excursion from Halifax in 1955. (F. Dean)

43

The once busy sidings by Blackpool's football ground at Bloomfield Road, with Black Five no 45377. (Author's collection)

followed in 1863, and was built as the terminus of the independent Blackpool & Lytham Railway, absorbed in 1871 by the LNWR and LYR. The station was originally named Blackpool (Hound's Hill) and then Blackpool Central in 1876. The line between Preston and Kirkham was quadrupled in 1889, Central station rebuilt in its final form in 1901, and the 'New Line' (or 'Marton Line') opened two years later. This additional line from Kirkham was built for express traffic and shortened the distance to Preston by five miles, allowing for the vast increase in passenger traffic in the first half of the 20th century. In the 1930s it was claimed that rail passengers to Blackpool and adjacent resorts totalled almost six million a year, and on Saturday, 18th July 1936 a record 656 trains passed Kirkham en route to and from Blackpool.

As well as the holiday traffic and regular services to Preston, Manchester, Liverpool and even London, an interesting aspect was the development of the Club carriage. This was the brainchild of Harold Bowman of St Annes and was a 'superior' first-class carriage attached to a residential (as distinct from holiday) express. It was reserved for the members of an exclusive group of businessmen, originally 50 in number. The first such carriage was provided by the LYR for the Blackpool Central to Manchester Victoria service in 1895, soon followed by the LNWR from Windermere and Llandudno to Manchester, and the Midland from Morecambe to Bradford. The LMS inherited all these services in 1923 and extended them, so that by 1939 there were four Blackpool to Manchester morning expresses with Club carriages, with the equivalent four return journeys in the evening. Use of the ex-LYR Dobbs Brow route to bypass Bolton meant that times for these expresses were as fast as a little over one hour for the journey from Manchester. Club services did not long survive World War II and nationalisation, although there was a limited revival of the scheme in the 1990s.

LMS Ivatt class 2F 2-6-0 no 6410 by the 'parachute' water tank on Central station's platform 3 in 1947 (the world-famous Blackpool Tower is just visible at the left). (Author's collection)

45

Works' and societies' outings to Blackpool were once commonplace, as shown here by this 1954 excursion for Birmingham allotment gardeners, headed by Black Five no 45322. (T. Lewis/N.E. Preedy)

A £2 million scheme to redevelop Central station in 1940 never took place due to World War II, but 1945 saw a return to pre-war boom days, and almost two million excursion passengers arrived by train as late as 1959. However, the policies of the Beeching years drastically reduced rail excursions, and the Beeching Report itself proposed that Blackpool North station should be closed and services to Central 'reorganised'. However, early in 1964 it was Central's closure that was announced. This was prompted as much by the value of the site as by reduced services, but whatever the motivation, the station and its multiple access lines from Blackpool South closed on Sunday, 1st November 1964 (at the end of the Illuminations). Even on that last day there had been 55 departures. Services on the 'New Line' to Blackpool South continued for another year, with excursion trains on the route until 1967. Now the resort is back to the original rail routes via Poulton and Lytham, though in 1985 Lancashire County Council proposed that the line between South and Central stations should be reinstated. Needless to say, this plan was never implemented, although there is still the intention to re-use the route for a 'light rail' link as part of the regeneration of the area's tramway system. After an undignified spell as a bingo hall, Central station was demolished in 1972 and now all that remains is the toilet block, whose takings in 'coppers' were once said to have paid the rates bill for the entire station site!

4
Preston Lines

Preston to Longridge/The Whittingham Hospital branch/The ELR at Preston/Ribble Steam Railway

Crowds gather for the last visit of a passenger train to Longridge, north-east of Preston, in 1962. This was a RCTS railtour headed by ex-LNWR 0-8-0 freight loco no 49451. (H.C. Casserley)

Preston to Longridge

Preston's first railway was part of the future West Coast Main Line, built northwards from Wigan by the North Union Railway and opened in 1838. However, its second line was a small self-contained branch built for stone quarries and originally worked by horse traction! Longridge is a small town 6 miles north-east of Preston, whose fame in the 19th century lay in its quarries. These produced a type of building stone known as

48

ashlar, much in demand for harbours, churches and other public buildings. In 1835 horse and cart were the only means of getting the quarried stone to navigable water at Preston. That year the Preston & Longridge Railway Company was set up to build a railway to transport stone in horse-drawn wagons from Tootle Height Quarry above Longridge to a terminus at Deepdale Street in Preston. The line was laid on 18 inch square stone sleepers, and was completed in March 1839, although the first train did not run until May the following year. A passenger service of sorts was also provided, consisting of two trains each way on Wednesdays and Saturdays, with an intermediate 'stopping place' at Grimsargh.

In 1846 the Fleetwood, Preston & West Riding Junction Railway sought to use the route of the P&LR from Preston to Grimsargh as part of its ambitious plan to link Fleetwood with

Maudland Bridge over a disused section of the Lancaster Canal was the site of a station between 1856 and 1885. (Author)

49

Leeds and Bradford. Ultimately nothing came of the overall scheme, but its effects on the P&LR were considerable. By 1848 the line, leased to the FP&WRJR, was adapted for steam traction, and two years later it was linked to other railways, with a one mile connection largely through tunnels to the Preston & Wyre Railway at Maudland. At first this was only for goods trains, passenger services continuing to Deepdale Street, but amidst the chaos of the collapse and revival of the FP&WRJR, stations were opened in 1856 on the new link, at Maudland Bridge and Deepdale Bridge. The latter became the FP&WRJR's headquarters, Deepdale Street being relegated to goods duties.

The line now resembled a more conventional branch, with five trains each way on weekdays (four on Sundays) and the provision of additional stations. These were Gammer Lane in 1854 (known as Fulwood from 1856 and finally as Ribbleton

This 1854 station was formerly called Gammer Lane, then Fulwood, only becoming Ribbleton in 1900, thus dating this scene with its distinguished-looking employee to the early years of the 20th century. (Lens of Sutton, courtesy R.K. Blencowe)

The Ribbleton station building still stands, though with a change in occupancy of the platform! (Author)

from 1900) and an earlier Ribbleton, open only from 1863 to 1866 but then used on occasions for the nearby Fulwood Barracks. However, in 1866 the original FP&WRJR scheme was revived, and fearing the Midland would gain access to Preston by this route, the LNWR and the LYR bought the Longridge branch and ran it as a joint concern until 1923. Improvements included a station building at Grimsargh (1870), ending the need to use a room at the Plough Hotel as a booking office at a rent of £6 a year! Similarly the Towneley Arms at Longridge was bought so that a proper station could be built there. Most significantly, the layout at Maudland was changed in 1885, at last allowing trains to run into Preston station, and the closure of Maudland Bridge station.

   Little changed over the next 45 years, though the transport of stone declined and had virtually ended by 1918. In that year a proposal was made for a light railway to extend the Longridge line to Hellifield but nothing came of it. At the Grouping of 1923, the line was regarded as 'quite healthy', with seven trains each way on Mondays to Fridays, with four extra on Saturdays and four Sunday trains. However, services were soon run down, Sunday trains ending in the late 1920s, followed by the closure of all regular passenger services in 1930. The last train was the 10 pm departure from Longridge on May 31st, complete with a wreath on the loco and a blessing from a local clergyman. The scene was described as resembling that of the first engine-hauled service of 1848, with crowds lining all the local bridges and fences. Annual Sunday School outings continued until 1939, and occasional railtours reached Longridge. The last of these was in 1962, when damage to points locked for the weekend probably ensured there were no further trips.

Another railtour visitor to Longridge was Fowler class 4P no 42316 on the 'North Lancashire' trip of May 1954. (Author's collection)

Here no 42316 takes on water at Longridge station. (B. Hilton)

Goods traffic continued to the mills and gasworks of Longridge until November 1967, when the line was cut back to the Courtaulds works at Red Scar. This was the largest man-made fibres plant in Europe when opened in 1938, with the county's tallest factory chimneys at 385 ft (known locally as the 'Preston Twins'). It also had its own two saddle tank locos, one of which, *Caliban*, is now on the Lakeside & Haverthwaite Steam Railway. By 1970 it was down to a single Sentinel loco and one coal train a day, and ten years later the works, and the rail line to it, closed completely. All that was then left of the former P&LR was a Y-shaped spur from Maudland to the original terminus in Deepdale Street. This served the coal depot for the whole of the Preston area and was still receiving daily coal trains in 1988, before going out of use in the early 1990s. Now the coal depot site and its rail link through the tunnels lie abandoned, though still with level crossing gates in place on two Preston streets.

Longridge station building also still stands, with part of its original canopy intact, and is used by local organisations. (Author)

Further out, the P&LR route is an official footpath through much of north-east Preston, and the 1854 station building eventually known as Ribbleton, still stands. The route through Grimsargh is also a footpath, while at Longridge the 40 yard Stonebridge tunnel is intact though sealed off. Most of the line through the town has been built over, but to the north an embankment is walkable out to the quarries. Nearby, a fine 'P&LR 1839' keystone is over the western entrance to the 55 yard tunnel under Higher Road. The town still has its former station building on Berry Lane, in good condition and used by local organisations.

The Whittingham Hospital branch

Free travel for passengers! Perhaps the destination stopped the offer being oversubscribed as this was uncompromisingly titled the Lancashire County Mental Asylum. Originally the residence

The Whittingham Hospital line's two locos in 1951, with the ex-Southern Railway engine at the right, and the earlier 1904 purchase clearly designated No 2 for the County Mental Hospital Works. (H.C. Casserley)

The hospital station was built on a curve, with a glass canopy over the single track, as seen here in 1951. (H.C. Casserley)

of the Waring family, it was enlarged in 1879 to take 2,895 patients. Access proved difficult for staff and visitors as well as patients, and so in 1884 the Hospital Management Committee suggested a 2 mile line from the former P&LR line at Grimsargh. The LNWR/LYR refused to build or operate the branch, but granted junction facilities, so the committee decided to go ahead with its own private line. After a delay due to opposition from local landowners, work began in 1887 and was completed two years later at a cost of £14,000. The original plans were for horse-working, but a Barclay 0-4-0 saddle tank had been purchased in time for the first train in June 1889. This hauled a single coach between rudimentary stations at Grimsargh and the hospital, where a goods shed and small engine shed were also provided.

A second loco was purchased in 1904, and three 4-wheeled carriages added to the stock. By 1918 about 3,000 passengers a week were being carried on nine trains daily (except Sundays), timed to fit in with Preston-Longridge services at Grimsargh. A 500 metres extension was added at the hospital in 1921, to give access to the boiler house. When the Longridge passenger trains ended in 1930, the Whittingham service (known locally as 'Sylum Billie') continued, adjusting its operation to bus times at Grimsargh. By 1945 maintenance arrears meant the stock had to be replaced and an ex-Southern Railway D1 tank (built at Brighton in 1886) was purchased, along with three ex-LNWR brake vans. These were converted for passenger use by the hospital joiners, fitted with gas lighting, and painted green. Services continued into the 1950s, though mostly for coal supplies to the hospital. A Sentinel steam shunter was bought from Bolton Gasworks in 1953, and three years later it was the only engine in service. The last passenger trains were in June 1957, with a special trip for rail society enthusiasts, prior to the final day of service on the 29th, though the last engine over the line ran ten months later. Then track was lifted, the stations demolished and a ½ mile cutting filled in. Otherwise the route can still be traced across the fields to the hospital.

The ELR at Preston

The Blackburn & Preston Railway was set up to link those two towns and construction started in 1844, but the following year it was absorbed by the East Lancashire Railway (ELR). The line was completed in 1846 and is still operational today. However, its approach to Preston between 1850 and 1972 is now abandoned and is dealt with here. At the outset, Preston Corporation objected to a second railway bridge over the Ribble, the river already being crossed by the North Union Railway (NUR) from Wigan in 1838 (the present West Coast Main Line crossing). This forced the ELR to use a longer route joining the NUR at Farington, 2½ miles south of Preston. Obstructive tactics by the NUR soon made the ELR again seek its own access to the town. Despite opposition, the ELR did get Parliamentary approval in 1847, but with a couple of

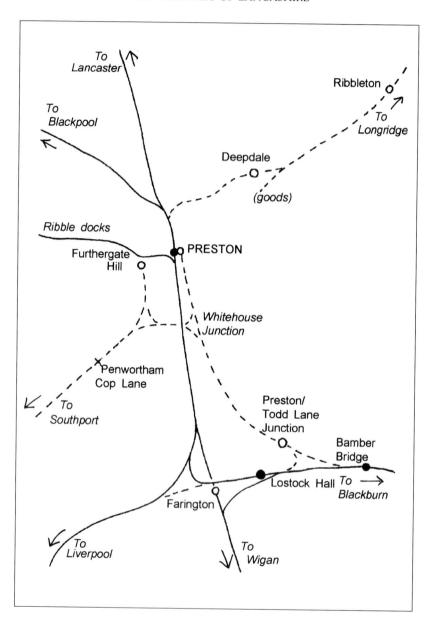

interesting provisions. One was that the new bridge over the Ribble would include a public footway, and a second provided for Preston Corporation to incorporate the embankment north of the river into a public park.

The new line ran from the station at Bamber Bridge, across the Ribble to the NUR's Preston station, which was extended to the east, including a new entrance for the ELR in Butler Street. One new station was also provided on the branch in 1852, misleadingly named Preston Junction. This was at a connection westwards to the former Liverpool, Ormskirk & Preston Railway (then part of the ELR) at Lostock Hall. Considerable construction difficulties were encountered at the Ribble crossing. The plan was for a 52-arch brick viaduct leading to a further two brick arches and three iron spans over the river. However, in October 1849, when the line was ready for opening, thirteen arches of the viaduct collapsed after the Ribble flooded. They were rebuilt in time for the line to be eventually opened in 1850, but proved such a problem following further floods that the whole viaduct was replaced by an embankment, completed in 1886.

The new line settled down to an 80 year existence, essentially for traffic from East Lancashire to Preston and the Fylde. It also initially provided for the Preston to Liverpool service, though after 1891 this used the newly constructed Farington curve instead. This loss of traffic was to some extent replaced by a new service in 1883 from Blackburn to Southport, which used a loop from Whitehouse Junction South to the Preston-Southport line (see Chapter 8). This had involved tunnelling below the six tracks of the main line without disturbing traffic. From 1900 an additional curve at Whitehouse Junction North allowed trains from Southport to reach the ELR side of Preston station. However, the mainstay of the ELR's Preston extension was the Blackburn to Preston service. In 1922 this consisted of 24–26 trains each way on weekdays, with 5–6 on Sundays.

In 1885 Preston Junction station was relocated 200 yards north of its original site, and in 1952 belatedly renamed Todd Lane Junction. Otherwise little changed until 1964, when the

Todd Lane Junction station (formerly Preston Junction) in July 1966, two years before closure, with Black Five no 44909. (Author's collection)

Whitehouse junctions shut, along with the line to Southport. Four years later the ELR line into Preston closed to passenger trains, followed in 1972 by final closure, along with the link west from Lostock Hall to Moss Lane Junction. (This had been used by trains from East Lancashire to gain access to the Preston to Liverpool line.) Closure included Preston station's former ELR platforms, though the Butler Street entrance lingered on until 1985. Nowadays, trains from Blackburn once more use the former NUR route into Preston.

Today, most of the former trackbed forms the Preston Junction Local Nature Reserve, giving access to the line from the A6 near Bamber Bridge to the River Ribble, including the spur to Lostock Hall and the lines from the Whitehouse junctions to Leyland Road. The reserve includes both sites of the former Preston Junction stations, with no remains at either. More interest is to be found at the northern end of the line. The bridge over the

The former East Lancs side of Preston station, with a local train headed by Stanier class 4P no 42460. (G. Harrop)

The view from the same spot today. The main train shed is still visible but the East Lancs part of the station has been replaced by car parking and a shopping centre. (Author)

The disused railway bridge for the East Lancashire line, with the Ribble at low water and the West Coast Main Line bridge in the background. (Author)

The bridge is still in use for pedestrians and is overlooked by the former Park Hotel, built by the LNWR and LYR in 1883. (Author)

Ribble (a 1930 replacement) still stands and can be crossed, though its safety may give some concern. The line can then be followed between Avenham and Miller Parks, with the former Park Hotel on the left. This was built by the LNWR and LYR jointly, and opened in 1883. It was connected to the station by its own footbridge and covered walkway to platform six. Vicar's Bridge still stands nearby, but instead of looking out over the former ELR tracks into the station, there is now only the view over a huge car park and shopping centre.

Ribble Steam Railway

This preservation project began with a different name and at a different location! 'Steamport' at Southport started in 1971 with an enthusiasts' organisation, which the following year took over the former LYR engine shed built in 1891 between Chapel Street and Central stations. This had closed in 1965 and was becoming derelict before its re-use as a transport museum. The formal opening was in 1975 and the museum continued as a successful operation into the 1990s. However, plans were underway for a wholesale redevelopment of the site and in 1997 the museum closed.

During the existence of 'Steamport', another Lancashire transport link had closed down. Preston's Prince Edward Albert Dock had opened in 1892 and at that time was the largest single dock in the country, with 1½ miles of quay and 28 miles of railway track. Trade continued to grow up to the peak year, 1968, when almost 2½ million tons of cargo were handled. However, keeping the river access free of silt had always been a problem and as dredging costs soared in the 1970s, trade declined rapidly and the dock closed for commercial shipping in 1981.

The port's rail link from the West Coast Main Line south of Preston station had dated back to 1846, built originally to serve Victoria Quay. In 1882 the dockside rail network was acquired by Preston Corporation which, following the dock's closure, completely re-routed the lines to serve industrial sites in the dock area, chiefly tar distillers. A new 'traditional LYR-style'

Preston Dock in 1967, with Bagnall 0-4-0T 'Energy'. The following year the corporation replaced these locos with Sentinel diesels. (J.A. Peden)

A very different scene in January 2003, with the dock used only for a marina at the far left, and its southern quayside now occupied by expensive housing. (Author)

engine shed was even built in 1985 to house three Sentinel 0-4-0 locos. At this time there were still two daily BR tanker trains to the complex, bringing Strand Road's traffic to a halt while they were waved across by two flagmen! To the relief of Preston's motorists these shipments ended in 1995, and the dock railway system became disused, but not forever.

The docks area had already seen some preserved steam activity as part of Preston Guild celebrations in 1992, and seven years later the former 'Steamport' organisation moved there under the new name of 'Ribble Steam Railway'. Since the move, much work has been done on the 1½ miles of track, plus structures including a museum, an engine shed and a 4-road workshop. Stock, with a concentration on ex-industrial locos, both steam

Open day at the Ribble Steam Railway workshop in January 2003, with at the right 'Progress', one of the surviving Sentinel diesel replacements for the Bagnall dock locos. (Author)

and diesel, has been acquired, and the line was formally opened for passenger services on 17th September 2005. By this time freight usage had also resumed, with three inbound bitumen trains each week for a local factory. In 2006 the passenger service operated each weekend from April to September, with Sunday trains in March and October, and 'Santa Specials' in December. Earlier that year, the railway had received an award from the Heritage Railway Association recognizing its unique status as Britain's only restored dock railway, and the progress made since 1999.

5
Into Yorkshire

Clitheroe to Hellifield/Colne-Earby-Skipton/
The Barnoldswick branch

Blackburn's fine LYR train sheds, now demolished, are seen behind Stanier
class 4P no 42624 with a train for Hellifield. (J. Davenport)

Clitheroe to Hellifield

The north-eastern boundary of Lancashire was changed in 1974
to include parts of the former West Riding of Yorkshire. This
chapter comprises three railways in this area, starting with the
line up the Ribble valley. Purists might object to the inclusion of
a line that is still in place, has scheduled summer 'specials', occasional steam railtours, and freight workings especially at its

67

southern end. However, regular passenger services ended in 1962 and have not been restored, despite the efforts of Ribble Valley Rail and other pressure groups. On these grounds it is included here as a 'lost' railway.

The Blackburn, Clitheroe & North Western Junction Railway was authorised in 1846 to build a line from the ELR at Daisyfield east of Blackburn to the proposed 'Little' North Western Railway at Long Preston. Work began the following year, but proceeded slowly due to financial problems and setbacks, including the death of three workers during the construction of the 48-arch Whalley viaduct. The line eventually opened as a single track to Chatburn, $1^3/_4$ miles past Clitheroe, with a ceremony on 20th June 1850. It was worked by the LYR from the start, and in 1859 it became the property of that company.

Jubilee no 45719 pauses at Chatburn station with a Blackburn-Hellifield train. (Author's collection)

A DMU on a 'Dalesrail' summer Sundays only service from Preston to Carlisle in July 2002 passes through Chatburn station, where the footbridge and canopy have gone but the building still stands. (Author)

Despite the original plans to continue to Long Preston, Chatburn remained the terminus for almost 30 years. It was only when the Midland began construction of the Settle & Carlisle line in 1869 that the LYR decided to extend the line to Hellifield, 1¼ miles east of Long Preston. The line to Chatburn was doubled in 1872, and the extension opened to Gisburn in June 1879, pending the completion of Hellifield station the next year. The 11½ mile line was first worked by the LYR, but in 1888 the Midland began running both passenger and goods services over the route and on to Manchester, with connections at Blackburn for Liverpool. By 1910 there were seven through weekday passenger trains each way over the line, though by 1934 there remained just one through service from Manchester to Glasgow, and even its carriages were usually attached at Hellifield to a train from Leeds.

69

To return to the closed section of the line, intermediate stations were built on the extension at Rimington, Gisburn and Newsholme. For much of the line's existence, local passenger services included trains from Manchester Victoria. At the start of services to Hellifield in 1880, eight out of the thirteen local weekday trains began at Manchester (three out of four on Sunday). In 1960, however, the line was down to a basic Blackburn to Hellifield service of six trains Monday–Friday, eight on Saturday, but no trains on Sunday. By then Newsholme and Rimington stations had closed (1957 and 1958 respectively). Gisburn and Chatburn, along with Clitheroe and all remaining stations along the line to Blackburn, closed on 10th September 1962.

In the 1980s pressure grew for a restoration of passenger services at least as far as Clitheroe, and this was achieved in May 1994. Now Clitheroe has an hourly weekday service to

The current terminus – Clitheroe – with a newly restored Sunday service to Manchester Victoria in July 2002 (the former station building on the right is now an art gallery). (Author)

Preserved LMS Stanier 4-6-2 no 6201 'Princess Elizabeth' was kept busy during 2002, the Queen's Golden Jubilee Year, with three trips over the Clitheroe-Hellifield line. (Author's collection)

Blackburn, Bolton and Manchester (two-hourly on Sunday). No such restoration has occurred for the line beyond Clitheroe, although it does have summer 'Dalesrail' trains. These began in 1975 with once-a-month services and now operate from Blackpool and Preston to Carlisle every summer Sunday, though no stops are made between Clitheroe and Hellifield. Some use of the line has continued for freight, particularly at the southern end, where the Horrocksford branch, also opened in 1850, gives access to the Castle Cement works. In 2007 no coal was brought in by rail, but rail-bourne cement traffic out from the works was due to resume later that year. In addition, there are freight trains at night over the line, while it continues to be used for both passenger and freight train diversions during work on the West Coast Main Line. Thus at least some rail staff and passengers still see the ornamental tunnel portals at Gisburn Park, the viaducts over Swanside Beck and Stone Beck, and the stationmasters' houses at Chatburn, Rimington, Gisburn and Newsholme, although only Chatburn retains its station building.

Colne-Earby-Skipton

Despite Colne's long-standing status within Lancashire (unlike many of the places in this chapter), its first railway arrived from Yorkshire. In 1848 the Leeds & Bradford Extension Railway (L&BER) built a line from Skipton to Colne, where it was joined the following year by the ELR from Accrington. The L&BER was already leased by the Midland Railway, which absorbed it in 1851, and by 1859 the ELR had been amalgamated with the LYR. Thus Colne station became a terminus for two separate railway systems, with 'All change!' a constant refrain across its three platforms, although two of these did allow through trains. In 1850 there were five weekday trains from Leeds to Colne, with connections on to Liverpool, but by then any hopes of a line as a major trans-Pennine route had been dashed by the opening of the much more direct Standedge line.

In 1876 the LYR began running trains through to Skipton, and the 1881 timetable showed ten weekday passenger trains from

Colne to Skipton, four operated by the LYR. Even at this time excursion traffic was important. Not only were there local and West Yorkshire trains to Blackpool, but also trips the other way, to York Races, the Yorkshire Dales, Morecambe and the Lake District, all via Skipton. In 1887 agreement was reached whereby LYR coaches would be hauled by Midland engines, so that in general services into Yorkshire remained the preserve of the Midland. The timetable for 1922 showed eleven Midland departures for Skipton most weekdays, with three on Sundays. There were two intermediate stations within present-day Lancashire, at Foulridge and Earby, though the line had closed by the time Earby was included in Lancashire, as part of the reorganisation of 1974 (two further station sites at Thornton and Elslack have remained within Yorkshire).

The pattern of largely local Skipton to Colne services, with through freight and holiday workings, continued through LMS

A snowy scene at Earby in February 1955 as no 42153, previously seen at Fleetwood, approaches from Skipton, with a Barnoldswick train waiting at the right. (Author's collection)

73

days, though under British Railways there were more regular through services. In summer 1959, for example, there were seven weekday trains from Skipton through Colne – one to Accrington, one to Liverpool, two to Manchester and three to Blackpool. On Saturdays there were three more scheduled trains through to Manchester and one to Stockport, and of course many more holiday specials heading to and from the Lancashire coast, including a regular West Hartlepool to Blackpool service known as the 'Saltburn'. During the local July holiday fortnight some specials headed in the opposite direction to the Yorkshire resorts.

The Liverpool to Skipton summer service was worked from Midge Hall near Leyland by crews from Lostock Hall engine shed. Joe Booth, then a fireman there, remembers the first summer working of 1963. At Midge Hall the Skipton portion (known as the 'Skipton Flyer') was detached from the through

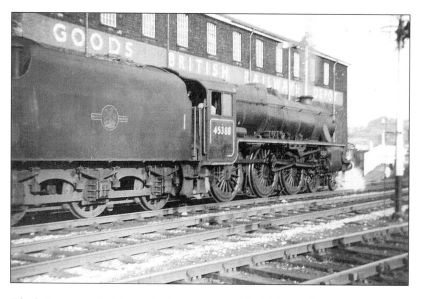

Black Five no 45388 by Colne's now-demolished Midland goods warehouse, in the 'last week of steam', August 1968. (J. Booth)

74

Liverpool to Glasgow train. Usually this consisted of three coaches, which could be handled by a small loco such as the class 2MT. However, on this occasion the Skipton portion was seven corridor coaches, for which the 2MT was anything but a 'flyer', slowing to walking pace on Hoghton Bank west of Blackburn and making a very late arrival at Skipton. Subsequently the larger Black Five locos were allocated to this trip.

Local provision meantime declined with the closure of Elslack station in 1952, and Foulridge seven years later. Diesel units were introduced for local passenger workings in 1960, and the next year for a Skipton to Manchester service every two hours. The Colne to Skipton line itself was spared in the Beeching cuts of 1963, though the passenger service was reduced and closures elsewhere had an adverse effect. The West Hartlepool to Blackpool summer Saturday service ended, and more crucially Colne lost its direct services to Manchester via Accrington (including those from Skipton). By the end of 1966 freight services between Colne and Skipton had virtually ended, and although the line's future appeared to be safe in a White Paper of 1967, the next year it was omitted from a list of lines to be subsidised. Consequently the line was closed on Monday, 2nd February 1970, which meant the last service train was the previous Saturday's 8.59 pm from Skipton to Manchester. However, the next day a special ran over the line to Colne and back, the points at Skipton being removed as soon as it had passed.

The station at Colne was demolished by September 1971, and all that is left is a single platform with a shelter. Gone are the Midland station building of 1883, the two engine sheds (one each for the Midland and the LYR), the goods and carriage sheds. At least what is left of a train service to Colne seems secure – an hourly service to Blackpool South. The trackbed to Skipton is reasonably intact as far as Thornton, though overgrown and flooded in places. It is scheduled to be used for an A56 bypass from Colne to Kelbrook and then from Earby to Thornton. Physical remains in situ are limited to the former goods shed at Earby, and station house plus platform at

Colne station in March 1955, with push-pull fitted ex-LYR Aspinall 2-4-2T no 50648 on the 'Puffing Billy' local service from Rose Grove. (Real Photographs)

Forty-seven years later, Colne station (one platform and a shelter) with the 12.55 pm arrival from Blackpool South. The buffers visible just beyond the train seal off the former route to Earby and Skipton. (Author)

Earby's former Midland goods shed still survives alongside an overgrown stretch of trackbed. (Author)

Thornton, but two remnants of the line are in use elsewhere. The station building at Foulridge was removed stone by stone and re-erected at Ingrow on the Keighley and Worth Valley Railway, while the signal box from Earby Gates level crossing is at Damems on the same line.

The Barnoldswick branch

Entirely within Yorkshire during its working life, but now in Lancashire, this 1¾ mile single-track branch ran from Earby to the small manufacturing town of Barnoldswick (known locally as 'Barlick'). It was built by the independent Barnoldswick Railway Company and opened in 1871. From the start it was operated by the Midland, starting with eight weekday trains to and from Earby. The line's junction only faced Earby so there

77

BR Ivatt class 2MT 2-6-2T no 41273 with a Barnoldswick train at Earby in March 1955. (J.A.G.H. Coltas)

BR Standard class 2MT 2-6-0 no 78036 arrives at Earby to take a railtour onto the Barnoldswick branch in September 1962. (A. Haynes)

were no services from the Colne direction. No intermediate stations were built but the terminus boasted a passenger station, goods shed, coal yard and even a tiny engine shed. The Midland bought the line in 1899 and increased the frequency of the service to Earby, called locally the 'Barlick Spud' – apparently from Spud Roaster! In 1922 there were twelve trains each way on weekdays with two on Sundays (down from six before the First World War). By the late 1950s the Sunday service was no more and the weekday trains were down to just one morning train to Skipton, returning in the late afternoon. This lingered on into the 1960s, but it was no surprise that the line was to be a Beeching casualty. The last passenger train ran on Saturday, 25th September 1965, with the goods service lasting until August 1966. The line can still be seen curving away from the former Skipton to Colne line south of Earby, but all traces in Barnoldswick have disappeared.

6
Around Accrington

The Great Harwood Loop/Stubbins to Accrington

Padiham station was still in use for Wakes Weeks specials at the time of this photo (1962), although this is a railtour headed by Crab no 42844, built at Horwich in 1930. (G. Harrop)

The Great Harwood Loop

This 9 mile branch to the north of Accrington, also known as the North Lancashire Loop, was built by the LYR between 1870 and 1877. Schemes involving the route had begun much earlier, in 1846, and keeping out rivals was one of the LYR's chief concerns. By taking a more northerly route between Blackburn and Burnley, through the small mill towns of Great Harwood and Padiham, the LYR was also able to ease congestion at Accrington with little increase in distance. However, it had reckoned without the construction difficulties which made this, for its length, probably the most expensive line built by the LYR. As well as the magnificent Martholme viaduct, whose ten arches carried the line 75 ft above the River Calder, lengthy embankments were required east of Great Harwood in an area affected by old coal workings. These proved so unstable that west of Padiham the line's opening had to be delayed until June 1877 for goods and October 1877 for passengers. Similar services east of Padiham had begun in July 1875 and September 1876 respectively.

The line left the Blackburn-Accrington-Burnley line at Great Harwood Junction and passed through several cuttings just to the north of Rishton where no station was provided. Stations were built at Great Harwood, at Simonstone (one of the smallest on the LYR system and known locally as 'Lamp-oil Junction'!) and the largest at Padiham. The line also served brickworks, collieries, gasworks and most importantly the power stations at Padiham (1926/7 onwards) before descending to rejoin the 'main line' at Padiham Junction. This was also known as Rose Grove West Junction; Rose Grove station and its more famous steam loco shed were just to the east.

Passenger services began in 1876 with eleven trains daily to and from Padiham, and stayed busy right up to 1939, when there were 18–19 trains each way on weekdays (5–6 on Sundays). By 1950 these had declined to 9–11 trains on weekdays, with no Sunday service, and six years later British Railways applied to close the line to passengers, claiming losses of almost £10,000 annually. Closure came in 1957, the last train being the 10.47 pm from Blackburn to Burnley on 30th November. This was the usual 2-4-2T hauling three carriages with only six passengers, two of whom had missed their connection for Colne!

However, this was not the end of the line's use as it had long been important for holiday traffic from Yorkshire and East Lancashire bound for Blackpool, which continued after the loss of ordinary passenger services. Indeed Great Harwood and Padiham stations reopened for two Wakes Weeks each year up to

81

Another railtour visit to Padiham, this time BR Britannia class 4-6-2 no 70015 'Apollo' in 1967. Later that year the station was demolished. (J. Davenport)

1963, when Padiham, for example, had two trains to the Yorkshire coast and one to North Wales. A second-class return fare to either Bridlington or Llandudno cost 33 shillings. In 1964 the final through holiday trains ran, along with the last of the local goods trains, and the western section of the line closed completely. To the east the line remained in use to Padiham 'B' power station, at first for coal trains, then for shipments of oil. When these stopped in 1991, the rest of the line was abandoned. Two years later, the power station itself closed and was subsequently demolished.

Today, the western end of the branch, nearest to Blackburn, has been lost beneath industrial estates, Blackburn's outer ring road and farmland. North of Rishton, the route is now a footpath, although the trackbed has been extensively landscaped in places. Great Harwood station site is now industrial units, but there is still Station Road, where the first house was formerly the stationmaster's residence. East of Great Harwood, the line between Mill Lane and Martholme Lane is used as a footpath. This leads

A Blackpool excursion headed by Black Five no 45205 pulls into Great Harwood in July 1962 (the station was still open for such holiday traffic). (G. Robinson)

A very different scene at Great Harwood station site only three years later. (G. Robinson)

The 10-arch Martholme viaduct survives, but is now closed to walkers as well as trains. (Author)

to the splendid Martholme viaduct, which was formerly accessible but is now securely fenced off. Through Simonstone the line is visible but not walkable, due to the demolition of bridges, and all that is left of Simonstone station is a very dilapidated goods shed. By Padiham, the single-track line for the power station was still in place in 2006, though much overgrown. This continued right through the town, where bridges were still intact (though nothing remained of the station) and on to Padiham Junction with its decaying points and signals.

Stubbins to Accrington

Accrington's first railway was the Blackburn, Burnley, Accrington & Colne Extension, incorporated in 1845 and absorbed by the ELR the same year. Its Act was for a T-shaped

84

route from Stubbins, ¾ mile north of Ramsbottom (see Chapter 7), to Accrington, from where lines would head west to Blackburn and east to Colne. All three sections opened in 1848 (the eastern part initially only as far as Burnley), and while the lines both east and west of Accrington remain in service, the one built northwards from Stubbins is now a 'lost' railway. It was described as one of the most difficult lengths of railway in the country, due to its 'Alpine' nature. From Stubbins Junction, the railway climbed for 5 miles at an average 1 in 78 through Helmshore and Haslingden stations to a summit at Baxenden, 771 ft above sea level, where another station was sited. From here the line dropped at gradients as steep as 1 in 38 for 2¼ miles down to Accrington station – this was the notorious Baxenden Bank, known locally as 'Accrington Broo'.

The line was principally used by services from Manchester to Colne, using an east curve at Accrington station to link two sections of the original scheme, while the west curve onto the

A fine shot of Helmshore station looking south in the early years of the 20th century. (J. Ryan collection)

section to Blackburn was less used. The 1849 timetable showed seven trains per day on weekdays from Colne to Manchester, with six the other way (four and three on Sundays). Following the amalgamation of the ELR and LYR in 1859, the line gained much use as an alternative to the congested LYR main line through Summit tunnel, with goods trains from the Todmorden to Burnley line, or even from the Midland line to Colne. It was also much used for holiday traffic, which provided the line's worst disaster in 1860, when a series of three LYR excursion trains were returning to Burnley and Colne. Twelve carriages of the second train broke loose and ran back down the line, colliding with the third train near Helmshore station. Eleven passengers died and over sixty were injured.

The Manchester service remained the mainstay of the line with 14 weekday trains from Colne in 1882, especially popular on Tuesdays and Fridays when the directors of Colne's mills travelled to Manchester Royal Exchange to buy their cotton. In the early 20th century, several trains ran non-stop daily each way over this line, most notably the 4.25 pm from Salford, which covered the 29 miles to Burnley Barracks in 49 minutes despite a load of up to 10 coaches. There were still 13 Manchester to Colne trains on weekdays as late as 1959; however, in 1964 services were 'rationalised' so that it was no longer possible to travel direct from Manchester to Colne via Accrington. Two years later the Stubbins to Accrington line closed altogether, as recommended in the Beeching proposals, and the rails were lifted in 1970/71. Station closures had in fact begun much earlier with Baxenden in 1951, followed by Haslingden in 1960. Only Helmshore lingered on until the closure of the line itself.

Accrington station is no longer a junction, and now has only the two platforms for trains between Blackburn and Burnley. No trace remains of the curve onto the Stubbins line or the platforms and original buildings of the ELR. The first ¼ mile of the route has also disappeared but is then visible as an embankment approaching Nuttall Street. On the other side of the street is the start of the concessionary footpath up the former Baxenden Bank. Climbing almost 200 ft over the next 1½ miles, this gives

Accrington station in 1950. At the extreme left are the surviving ELR buildings of 1848, with the lines to Stubbins swinging left. Lines to Blackburn are at the right, and in the background is the LYR station building of 1882. (Stations UK)

A very different scene at Accrington in 2002, with a Leeds to Blackpool North train leaving one of the two remaining platforms. (Author)

Most of the former rail route up Baxenden Bank is now a footpath, here seen with some of Accrington's surviving textile mills. (Author)

an excellent impression of the difficulties faced by loco crews. A further ½ mile of unofficial footpath leads to the site of Baxenden station, where only the southbound platform can still be found in the undergrowth.

The line on from Baxenden has been lost to factories, infilling and the A56 road, which has taken its route round Haslingden, obliterating all signs of the railway and Haslingden station. It reappears at the former crossing of the B6232, where bridge abutments remain, and can be walked for ¾ mile past the Museum of the Lancashire Textile Industry at Helmshore, although the viaduct over the River Ogden has been demolished. Helmshore station has retained its stationmaster's house and a stone replica of the signal box, but the trackbed through the site and on to Lumb is inaccessible. Fine viaducts remain, however, at Raven Shore and Lumb. Just past the second of these, a final ¾ mile is walkable, and has been resurfaced as part

The stationmaster's house and a version of the signal box are to be seen at the site of Helmshore's former level crossing. (Author)

of a national cycle trail. This leads over one of the two viaducts at Alderbottom, the lower one being used by the East Lancashire Railway (see Chapter 7), whose tracks run parallel with the disused line to the junction at Stubbins.

7
Rossendale Routes

Bury to Bacup/The Holcombe Brook branch/
The 'new' East Lancashire Railway/
Rochdale to Bacup

Typical Rossendale scenery surrounds the former trackbed of the Rochdale to Bacup line at Britannia, now used as a footpath. (Author)

Bury to Bacup

Rossendale, or more correctly the Forest of Rossendale, is a hill area in the east of Lancashire. It contains the source of the River Irwell, which flows west and south through several small manufacturing towns, chiefly Bacup, Rawtenstall and

Ramsbottom, in a deep but often narrow valley. The Manchester, Bury & Rossendale Railway was set up in 1843 to build a line from Clifton, 5 miles north-west of Manchester, following the valley up to Rawtenstall. However, before construction began two years later, the company had become the ELR, and an extension to Accrington had been promoted from Stubbins, north of Ramsbottom, so much of the original proposal became a branch line, later extended up the valley to Bacup. This section covers the line between Bury, Stubbins and Rawtenstall, plus the Bacup extension. The line between Clifton and Rawtenstall was opened in 1846, with five trains each way on the Bury to Rawtenstall section (four on Sundays). From Bury Bolton Street, stations were provided at Summerseat, Ramsbottom, Stubbins, Ewood Bridge (with a short-lived horse-bus service to Haslingden) and Rawtenstall. Keeping to the Irwell valley was not always straightforward, as the river had to be crossed nine times. In addition the Bury to Ramsbottom section required lengthy viaducts to stay above marshy ground, and tunnels to cut through spurs at Brooksbottoms and Nuttall.

Meanwhile, the route from Rawtenstall to Bacup was surveyed in 1845 and construction began two years later, coming to a temporary halt beyond Waterfoot, where a station was built, originally called Newchurch. Services began in March 1848, but it was another four years before they reached Bacup. The problem was a particularly narrow section of the Irwell valley just past Newchurch, known locally as the Glen. The road through had been built on a ledge cut out of the rock, and the only way left for the railway was by tunnelling. The single-track line was carried through the obstruction by two tunnels, Newchurch No 1 and No 2. Once past these, progress to Bacup was relatively easy, though six more crossings of the Irwell (raising the total from Bury to 22) and a further tunnel were needed. There was another station at Stacksteads before the terminus at Bacup, at 800 ft the highest station on the ELR. By 1857, increased traffic meant the line needed to be doubled between Stubbins and Rawtenstall but completion of the Rawtenstall to Bacup section (where a station was added at Clough Fold in 1871) waited until

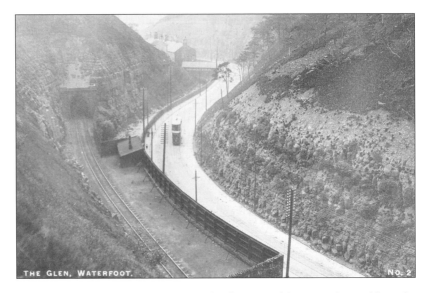

The narrow defile of the Glen is clearly shown in this 1913 view, with to the left the opening between Newchurch tunnels 1 and 2, and in the centre a Rawtenstall tram bound for Bacup. (J. Ryan collection)

1881. The problem was again at the Glen, where enlarging the two earlier tunnels was ruled out in favour of a parallel 592 yard tunnel. This was to be Newchurch No 3 but the navvies' name for it – the Thrutch – became the accepted one.

The line settled down to a steady existence as part of a Bacup to Manchester service, originally via Clifton, then via Prestwich from 1879, and finally via Heywood and Castleton from 1916. Most passengers for Manchester after that date changed onto the electric service at Bury, and eventually most Bacup trains terminated there. Railmotor services were introduced in 1914 for the Bacup to Ramsbottom trains, known locally as 'Little Billie'. These continued until 1948 (the last ex-LYR railmotors in service). Push-pull fitted 2-4-2 tank locos took over for the last years of steam passenger trains. In November 1954 the *Northern Daily Telegraph* had a headline 'Diesel Train Has Trials In Valley',

This fine LYR goods warehouse at Waterfoot was built in 1880 and is now owned by a road haulage firm. (Author)

The late afternoon freight to Moston sidings at Manchester is seen here with ex-LMS class 7F 0-8-0 no 49666 at Ramsbottom in May 1955. (B. Roberts, courtesy J.A. Peden)

Ex-LYR 2-4-2T no 50829, fitted for push-pull working, approaches Bacup from Bury in August 1953. (J. Davenport)

referring to lightweight diesel multiple units, and these trains were introduced in February 1956. There were 35 trains each way per day, giving a half-hourly service to Bury, the most frequent ever seen on the line. It is surprising that this did not survive the Beeching cuts, but over-manned stations, loss-making goods facilities and reduced passenger numbers (due in part to successive fare increases) made it easy to present a case for closure. This came for passenger services to Bacup in 1966, with the last train – packed with enthusiasts and local people – the 11.45 pm from Rawtenstall on Saturday, 3rd December and its return from Bacup after midnight. Passenger trains from Bury to Rawtenstall lasted another six years.

As well as regular services, the line had been busy with 'specials', and not just the annual Wakes Weeks trains in the last week of July (often involving double-headed trains of 10–12 coaches from Bacup). Autumn excursion trains ran to Blackpool and Morecambe illuminations, plus football and race meeting specials, and school trips as far afield as Edinburgh and North

Stanier class 4P no 42644 at Bacup on the 'Rossendale Farewell' railtour organised to mark the last day of passenger services to that town – 3rd December 1966. (Author's collection)

Wales. There was also considerable goods traffic, particularly in the 19th century, transporting building stone from numerous sidings between Rawtenstall and Bacup. By 1905 goods traffic was more varied, with on most weekdays seven goods trains leaving Bacup. In the 1950s there was still a late afternoon freight train each weekday to sidings at Manchester, but the line beyond Rawtenstall closed to freight as well as passengers in December 1966. Rawtenstall's passenger services lingered on until 3rd June 1972 and a regular train serving a coal depot there ended in 1980, paving the way for the 'new' East Lancashire Railway.

The line beyond Rawtenstall was lifted in October 1968, and the first stretch east, past the town, has become a road. Much of the rest has disappeared beneath builders' yards, factory car parks etc. Nothing remains at any of the station sites, except for Waterfoot's goods warehouse. Bridge remnants are plentiful, most notably the seven stone arches of Hareholme viaduct west

95

Today both Newchurch No 1 and the Thrutch tunnels are sealed off, although Newchurch No 2 (not shown) is still walkable. (Author)

of Waterfoot – now a public footpath. The three Newchurch tunnels are still intact but two of them are sealed off, with only the 290 yards of No 2 tunnel open and walkable – a rather eerie experience!

The Holcombe Brook branch

This 4 mile single-track branch from the Bury to Ramsbottom line was built by the independent Bury & Tottington District Railway Company, but was operated from the start by the LYR. Despite opposition from the Earl of Derby, it was constructed between 1878 and 1882, with seven intermediate stations planned. Initially only those at Woolfold, Tottington and Greenmount were built, along with the terminus at Holcombe Brook. The line was not easy to build or work, with viaducts

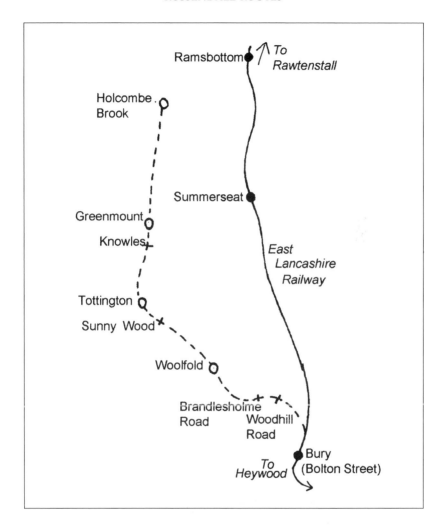

over the Irwell, the Kirklees Brook, and a mill lodge (reservoir) at Tottington, and gradients as steep as 1 in 40 as part of a steady 236 ft climb from Bury. Only a year after its completion, it faced competition from steam trams on the main road to Tottington, but it was their replacement by electric trams in 1904 that posed

The viaduct over the Irwell still stands and clearly shows pier bases built for the doubling of the track (which never happened). (Author)

more of a threat. In response, the LYR introduced its original Kerr Stuart railmotors on the line in 1905, with four additional halts at Woodhill Road, Brandlesholme Road, Sunny Wood and Knowles. These were just stopping points with no platforms or buildings. Services at this time were 21 return trips Monday to Friday, with an extra train on Saturday and eleven on Sunday.

Even so the line might have had a short life but for an early experiment with electrification. In 1913 Dick, Kerr & Co of Preston used the branch for an overhead line at 3,500 volts dc. This was the first application in the world of a high dc voltage for railway electrification. Although it had been provided free, the LYR bought the equipment in 1916, and the following year began converting it to 1,200 volts dc supplied by conductor rail, to fit in with the system already installed on the Manchester to Bury line via Whitefield. Brandlesholme Road and Sunny Wood

The simple terminus at Holcombe Brook on the penultimate day of passenger services, 4th May 1952, with a train from Bury hauled by ex-LYR 2-4-2T no 50651. (Author's collection)

halts were now provided with platforms and shelters, but Knowles and Woodhill Road closed (the latter eventually reopened in 1934). Services were maintained by the LMS, reaching a peak of 29 weekday trains in 1938, but by 1951 the system was ready for renewal. This was not thought to be worth the cost, and so for 14 months the line's passenger services reverted to steam traction, with a 2-4-2 tank loco and railmotor coach. This was only while British Railways applied to close the line, claiming this would save £12,357 per annum! The last passenger train was the 10.26 pm from Holcombe Brook on Sunday, 4th May 1952. Freight continued to Holcombe Brook until 1960, when goods services were cut back to Tottington. They finished completely in 1963, the line being lifted the following year.

The fine six-arch viaduct over the Irwell remains intact and is used for a cycle path, but the one over the Kirklees Brook has been demolished, cutting off the upper part of the line. Past this, about 1½ miles of trackbed can be walked through Tottington,

A fine close-up of 50651 at Holcombe Brook. This loco was built by the LYR in 1892 and not withdrawn until December 1955. (J. Davenport)

including the viaduct over the mill lodge. The walkable stretch ends at the site of Greenmount station, where nothing is left (as at all the other stations and halts). The final stretch to Holcombe Brook is now under housing and a small shopping precinct.

The 'new' East Lancashire Railway

On July 25th 1987, a 'new' East Lancashire Railway opened for passenger service, using 4 miles of its 19th century namesake's route along the Irwell valley from Bury to Ramsbottom. The East Lancashire Railway Preservation Society had begun the long quest to achieve this some 19 years previously and at a different location! The aim in 1968 had been to reopen part of the Stubbins to Accrington line (see Chapter 6) with Helmshore as the focus of operations. The station building was repaired, track (from a munitions depot at Standish) laid, and stock purchased

A 'celebrity' visitor to the East Lancashire line – LNER A3 4472 'Flying Scotsman' crosses Brooksbottoms viaduct in February 1993. (Author)

including two tank locos. However, purchase of a significant amount of trackbed proved impossible and at its annual general meeting in 1971 the society agreed to look elsewhere.

Various sites were considered, but in 1972 the former ELR goods shed at Castlecroft was leased from Bury Council. Both railway stock and preserved road vehicles were used to create a 'transport museum' there, while negotiations continued with British Railways over the use of the line to Rawtenstall. Two events in 1980 eventually made this possible. The first of these was the closure of the line itself, the second was BR's move away from Bury's Bolton Street station to a new bus and rail (now Metrolink) interchange, roughly on the site of the town's former Knowsley Street station. Now both the station – virtually intact following rebuilding in 1952 – and the line were available for the preservation project.

Another visiting 'star' – LNER A4 60007 'Sir Nigel Gresley' at Ramsbottom station in January 1988. (Jen Suggitt)

However, the reopening would not have been possible without the practical and financial help provided by the then Greater Manchester (now Bury) and Rossendale councils, keen on the scheme both for the use of local people and to promote tourism within the area. The councils purchased the route, track and structures, helped negotiate with other bodies and provided a wide range of services, with the society supplying much of the workforce. The original aim was to reopen in spring 1985, but it was two more years before this was possible and then only for 4 miles to Ramsbottom.

The opening day's six-coach train was hauled by two 0-6-0T locos, and from this start the society was able to maintain a regular Bury-Ramsbottom and return service on Saturdays and Sundays. As many as 35,000 passengers had been carried by the end of 1987. Meanwhile, work continued on the 4 mile extension to Rawtenstall, opened on April 27th 1991, with an intermediate halt at Irwell Vale (replacing an earlier station at Ewood Bridge). The next project was to reconnect the line to the national network via Heywood, using part of the former Bolton-Bury-Rochdale route closed to passenger services in 1970. This was made necessary by the conversion of the direct link from Bury to Manchester into a light rail route for Metrolink services, unusable by conventional railway stock from 1991. The connection was opened in 1993, but only for the movement of engines and rolling stock. After many delays, the 4-mile line between Bury and Heywood re-opened to passenger traffic on 6th September 2003.

By 2007 services comprised Heywood–Bury–Ramsbottom–Rawtenstall trains at weekends throughout the year, with a mixture of steam and diesel haulage on Saturdays, and all steam-hauled trains on Sundays. Additional services operated

Restored Crab no 42765 on the summer-only Friday service at the rebuilt Ramsbottom station in July 2001. (Author)

The line's diesel stock is here represented by class 31 D5600 passing Ramsbottom's 1938 LMS signal box in June 2002. The crossing gates were under repair at the time! (Author)

on Wednesdays, Thursdays and Fridays from May to mid-September. Special events have included steam, diesel and 'Thomas the Tank Engine' weekends, pullman-style dining trains and 'Santa Specials' – all helping to maintain the line's status as one of the UK's leading rail preservation schemes.

Rochdale to Bacup

The name 'New Line' is still used in the Bacup area for the route of a branch that opened over 120 years ago and has been closed for well over 50 years. This is because it was Bacup's second railway, opened almost 30 years after the ELR line from Bury. It was never a financial success, and was built despite strong opposition from within the company itself. This was the LYR, which constructed the line over 19 years between 1862 and 1881, chiefly to keep out the rival Manchester, Sheffield & Lincolnshire Railway. The line was first built from Rochdale to Facit, opening in 1870, and a second Act was required for the remaining 3½ miles to Bacup. Work on this section did not start until 1878, and the completed line finally opened in December 1881, without any formal ceremony.

There were considerable construction difficulties, starting at the Rochdale end with an impressive viaduct over the River Roch. The first station was Wardleworth, probably the busiest on the line as it was convenient for Rochdale town centre, and some Rochdale services from beyond this line terminated there to ease congestion at Rochdale station. The next station was at Shawclough, where the Turner Brothers asbestos works was a major user of the line from its opening in 1919. A 'double bridge' can still be seen nearby – a second one had to be built above the first after it slid down an unstable embankment. Further on was Healey Dell viaduct, with eight stone spans 105 ft above the River Spodden. The construction problems now eased, but the single-track line continued to climb at 1 in 60 through stations at Broadley, Whitworth and Facit, scene of the branch's worst accident. In 1891 an out of control stone train collided with a passenger train, killing two people. From here, the line was double-track on gradients of 1 in 40 past Shawforth station to the line's summit at 967 ft above sea level. This was the highest point on the whole LYR system, with weather to match – a passenger train was completely snowed under here in January 1940. Then came a rapid descent at 1 in 34 through Britannia station to Bacup.

Passenger services from Rochdale to Bacup began in 1881, but were soon affected by competition from trams which began running from Rochdale to Whitworth as early as 1884, and were extended to Bacup in 1911. Six years later, Britannia and Shawclough stations closed (though the latter reopened in 1919), and Sunday services ended in 1918. Weekday passenger trains over the whole line totalled eleven each way in 1922. Goods traffic was more successful, especially for stone quarried from the Rossendale hills and brought by incline down to the

Elderly ex-LYR locos at Bacup engine shed a year before its closure in 1954. (J.B. Hodgson)

The last railtours on the branch used ex-LYR 'Pug' 0-4-0ST no 51218, seen here at the site of Broadley station in February 1967, six months before the line closed completely. (Author's collection)

An original footbridge still spans the empty trackbed near Shawforth. (Author)

line between Britannia and Broadley. These worked later than most Rossendale stone quarries, and it was the closure of the last rail-worked quarry system in 1947 that brought the end of goods traffic over the severe gradients north of Facit. The same date, 16th June 1947, was used for the closure of the whole branch to passenger services, by then down to six trains daily.

The line itself was kept open to serve Bacup loco shed, built by the curve to the ELR line south of Bacup station. In 1921 thirty-seven locos were shedded there, but by 1954 this was down to eight and their departure to Bury that year meant the whole upper part of the line went out of use. Goods trains continued to reach Facit until 1963, and a daily coal train ran to Whitworth for another four years. A few railtour specials used the line while it remained open, latterly brake van trips using an ex-LYR 'Pug'. Most of the station sites are now unrecognisable, although the single platform remains at Broadley. The viaduct

107

The splendid viaduct at Healey Dell still soars 105 ft above the River Spodden. (Author)

over the Roch was demolished in 1972, almost inadvertently as a test explosion on one of the arches set off a chain reaction and eleven arches collapsed! The magnificent example at Healey Dell still stands and is the highlight of a 1½ mile walkable stretch of trackbed south of Whitworth. A similar distance can be walked through Shawforth and Britannia; although heavily landscaped in part, this section gives a good impression of the difficulties faced by this 'mountainous' line.

8
Lines At Southport

*Southport to Preston/The West Lancashire Light
Railway/Aintree to Southport/The Liverpool,
Southport & Preston Junction Railway*

*An atmospheric shot of Black Five no 44756 on the Southport to Preston
service in February 1964. (K. Hick)*

Southport to Preston

The seaside resort of Southport was first reached by rail from
Liverpool in 1848, and from the Wigan direction in 1855. Both of
these lines are still working, but as often happens it is the town's
later lines that have closed. The first of these to be built was the
West Lancashire Railway (WLR) to Preston, incorporated in

110

1871. Progress with construction was slow; the first section of 6½ miles from Hesketh Bank to Hesketh Park on the outskirts of Southport did not open until 1878. Later that year a temporary terminus for Southport opened at Windsor Road. This became known as Ash Street from 1882, when a proper terminus was provided at Derby Road (Southport Central), and was replaced by additions to the LYR's St Luke's station in 1902. Completion of the northern end was just as slow, the line being extended first to Longton in 1882 (Longton Bridge from 1892), then to a new Preston station at Fishergate Hill later that year.

The line ran through a thinly populated market-gardening area and traffic was sparse. As well as those already mentioned, stations were provided at Churchtown, Crossens, Banks, Hundred End, River Douglas (1882–7) and Hoole. Services

Banks station on the last day of service, 6th September 1964, with the original WLR station building to the right and a more recent house for the station-master at the left. (Author's collection)

Stanier 4P no 42439 crossing the River Douglas in 1963. The bridge had been built to swing open for river traffic but, from the 1880s, remained fixed in position for trains. (B.G. Barlow/J.A. Peden, courtesy K. Hick)

were initially 15 trains each way daily (five on Sundays), but the line was little used as it had no links with any others. This was particularly the case at Preston where Fishergate Hill was well away from the main station and town centre, despite the provision of a tramcar service. The first link to other companies came in 1883 with a loop onto the former ELR at Whitehouse Junction, allowing Blackburn to Southport services. An additional station was provided at Howick in 1889 (Hutton & Howick from 1898, New Longton & Hutton from 1924), but more interesting was the Tarleton branch. This ran from Hesketh Bank alongside the River Douglas for a little over a mile, and was built privately by Sir Thomas Hesketh in 1880. The same year it was sold to the WLR, who used it with steamship services along the river and on to Liverpool. The company also ran the paddle steamer *Virginia* across the Ribble to Lytham for a time when the River Douglas station was open.

The WLR never paid a dividend and was soon bankrupt. It limped on as an independent concern until 1897 when it was absorbed by the LYR, who were worried that it might be used to give the Manchester, Sheffield & Lincolnshire Railway access to Blackpool. The new owner soon completed the Whitehouse junction to give the line access to the main Preston station. By 1901 both WLR termini had been relegated to goods duties, trains by then running into the LYR's Chapel Street station at Southport. (Fishergate Hill was brought back into service for the Preston Guild celebrations of 1902 and 1922.) Now holiday trains from Scotland (as well as those from East Lancashire) could use this route to Southport, and from 1911 to 1913 the line saw a summer express service from Liverpool Exchange to Blackpool Central. However, it remained basically a country branch, with a limited amount of commuter traffic at each end, a halt being added at Cop Lane (Penwortham) in 1911. A

The West Lancashire Railway's first Southport to Crossens service was worked by three of these tiny 0-4-0 tank locos built by Kitsons of Leeds in 1884. (J.A. Peden collection)

113

railmotor service was introduced the next year from Crossens to the Tarleton branch, where halts were opened for the village and at Boatyard Crossing. This, however, only lasted for 16 months, although the branch continued in use for freight until 1930.

More successful was the Southport to Crossens electric train service. This began in 1904 as an extension of the LYR Merseyside third-rail (650v dc) electrification – the first of a standard line in this country. Expresses from Liverpool to Southport ran on as stopping trains to Crossens, giving an initial service of 17 trains a day. From 1909, most trains also included Meols Cop, which involved reversing out of that station and the service became Southport (Chapel Street) to Crossens via Meols Cop. After 1914 this was largely worked by lightweight multiple units originally designed for the Liverpool Overhead Railway and known locally as 'orange-boxes' (from their wooden seating

From 1904 to 1964 electric units worked the Southport to Crossens service, such as these seen at Hesketh Park station in 1962. (K. Hick)

114

Hundred End station, with a fine display of BR advertisements, shortly before closure in 1962. (K. Hick collection)

in third-class!). These lasted until 1945/6 when they were at last replaced by LMS stock. The Crossens electric service still provided 36 trains each way on weekdays in 1959 (down from a peak of 52 up to 1939), and Sunday services ended around this time.

Apart from the Tarleton branch, the 'West Lanky' survived with a service of around 15 trains each way daily (six on Sundays) until the Beeching era. Hundred End station, known locally as 'Celery Junction', had shut in 1962 and significantly the reason given for closure was the switch of market gardeners and farmers to road transport. The Beeching Report recommended closure of the whole line, and this was speedily implemented on 6th September 1964, when hundreds of people turned out to see the last trains, including 300 on the tiny platform at Hesketh Bank from where most of the protests against

115

Black Five no 44949 (previously seen at Morecambe) with a Preston to Southport train in June 1964, three months before the line's closure. Many other Lancashire lines had long been dieselised by then. (K. Hick)

closure had come. The electrics had ended the previous day with the 10.55 pm from Southport Chapel Street, thus giving the line as far as Crossens the dubious distinction of losing its two services on consecutive days!

Today little is left of the WLR. Both termini lingered on until the 1970s for other uses, but have since been demolished. All other stations have disappeared without trace. At Penwortham, the piers of the Ribble crossing remain, also embankments and bridge abutments at the junctions. Otherwise the trackbed is largely under housing at the Southport end, and under a new road approaching Preston, with farmland in between. All that remains is about 1,000 yards of track from the site of the original Windsor Road station to the former triangular junction at Meols Cop. This stretch is still in use for Southport to Wigan services, as the direct line through Blowick was removed in 1965.

The West Lancashire Light Railway

This project was first set up in 1967 by six schoolboy enthusiasts. Five of these are still active with the railway, one regularly crossing from USA (where he now lives) to help as a volunteer! The aim was the preservation of narrow gauge locos and rolling stock, little used for passenger carrying in Britain but widely employed for industry, mines, quarries etc. The first step was the laying of 150 yards of 2 ft gauge track round a flooded claypit by Alty's Brickworks, close to Hesketh Bank station on the former West Lancashire line.

In 1968 the first loco was acquired – *Clwyd*, a 1951 Ruston & Hornsby diesel from Burscough Brick and Tile Works Ltd, only 7 miles away. The next year, a second diesel followed from the same source, and a start was made on the steam loco collection. This was *Irish Mail* bought incomplete from the auction of stock

Ex-Spanish colliery loco 'Montalban' (built in Berlin in 1913) gets ready for operations at an enthusiasts' weekend in August 2002. (Author)

117

from the closure of Dinorwic Slate Quarry in North Wales. The main drawback was the lack of a boiler, and when a suitable one was found from a loco being dismantled for spares, it was at the top of Dinorwic Quarry, in a position most enthusiasts thought irretrievable. After 5½ months hard work in the summer of 1972, the group managed to get the boiler to where it could be collected and delivered to Hesketh Bank. Their troubles were not over, however, as a new inner firebox was needed, and it was 1980 before *Irish Mail* could be steamed.

Meanwhile the track was extended to 370 yards in 1970, and to its present 430 yards six years later. Passenger stock was built or converted, and an engine shed/workshop constructed. Most noticeable to visitors were the additions to the stock of locos including *Joffre*, a Kerr Stuart 0-6-0T built at Stoke in 1915 for the French army; *Montalban* and *Utrillas*, two steam locos from a

Becconsall station with ex-Welsh slate quarry loco 'Stanhope', built in 1917 by Kerr Stuart. (Author)

Spanish coal mine; *Stanhope*, a 1917 0-4-2T also built by Kerr Stuart but brought from Poland; and most recently a 1917 Henschel once used on sugar estates in Mozambique!

By 2007 the railway had 31 locos, 8 of them steam, though not all operational. The track consists of an L-shaped line round the claypit pond, from a station named Becconsall, with adjacent engine shed, workshop and stores, to Willow Tree and Delph halts. Track continues northwards for 200 yards but is not used at present. The line operates from Easter to the end of October, generally on Sundays only, plus Bank Holiday Mondays and occasional Saturdays, with special events including family days and enthusiasts' weekends. Trains carry up to 60 passengers and operate at 20-minute intervals. In early 2004 a new engine shed/paint shop was opened, and the railway hopes eventually to have a museum for its historic exhibits, and an extension to

Not all the line's stock was in such sparkling condition in August 2002, as seen by ex-Liverpool Waterworks Planet diesel, with ex-Polish 'Chrsanow' undergoing restoration. (Author)

more then double the existing track length. After over 30 years of operation, the line has established itself as a small but successful enterprise, and certainly one unique within North West England.

Aintree to Southport

By 1880 Southport already had three railway lines including one to Liverpool, completed to Exchange station in 1850 and run by the LYR. As the resort grew, its local worthies saw the Cheshire Lines Committee (CLC), which had reached Aintree by a 'loop line' through Liverpool's eastern outskirts in 1879, as the likely provider of a second link to the city. However, the CLC refused to become directly involved, agreeing only to work the line when constructed. Despite this, the CLC's name was included in the title of the Southport & Cheshire Lines Extension Railway

Ainsdale Beach station was the last to be built, in 1901. Nine years later its takings did not even pay the stationmaster's wages! (J.A. Peden collection, courtesy K. Hick)

120

(SCLER), a 14 mile double-track line following an inland route from Aintree to Ainsdale, then through the dunes to Southport. The line opened in 1884, with stations at Sefton & Maghull, Lydiate, Altcar & Hillhouse, Woodvale and Birkdale, before a magnificent terminus on Southport's Lord Street. Additional stations were opened at Barton & Halsall in 1886 (Mossbridge from 1894) and Seaside in 1901 (Ainsdale Beach from 1911).

It has been said that a route from Liverpool to Southport deliberately avoiding all major centres of population would probably resemble that of the SCLER. At a distance of 31 miles from central Liverpool, as compared to the LYR's 18½ miles, it could never compete with that company's direct coastal route. In fact its main use was for Manchester (Central) to Southport trains, with a service of nine trains each way daily on weekdays (three on Sundays) in 1909, plus numerous excursion trains during the summer. By 1888 the company was unable to pay its debts and a receiver was appointed. The situation was resolved by the CLC, which guaranteed further borrowing while still refusing to take over the railway completely, though there was a commitment to run the line in perpetuity.

Up to 1914 the line saw regular expresses from Manchester and Liverpool, and was particularly busy in the summer months, with as many as 50,000 passengers arriving at Lord Street station on bank holidays. However, its dependence on holiday traffic, rather than the local service, was emphasised during World War I when all stations, including Lord Street, were closed in January 1917. All except Mossbridge reopened in April 1919, and usage increased for a time. Services soon declined with expresses only on Saturdays, and stopping services from Gateacre on the CLC Liverpool Loop Line being handled by Sentinel steam railcars. The end of the line's nominal independence finally came with nationalisation in 1948, and services were further reduced. By 1950 there was only one express a week – Saturdays only from Stockport – and Lord Street station had only eight scheduled passenger trains on weekdays. In 1952 this railway became one of the first that had been built as a main line to close, for passengers in January and

Lord Street station looked reasonably busy in 1951, only a year before closure. (J.A. Peden collection, courtesy K. Hick)

The last passenger train to use the line was this railtour visit to Altcar & Hillhouse in 1959, with ex-LNWR class G2 49434. (J.A. Peden)

Southport's Lord Street station frontage is little changed today from its days as a rail terminus. (Author)

for goods six months later. The track was kept for freight north to private sidings at Altcar & Hillhouse until 1960, but then lifted.

Looking for what is left from south to north, nothing is to be seen at the site of Aintree Central, now an industrial estate, and the trackbed has been lost as far as Maghull. From there, 5½ miles have been made available for walkers and cyclists as the Cheshire Lines Path. This passes the sites of Lydiate, Altcar & Hillhouse and Mossbridge stations, all of which have left no trace. From the A565 into Southport, the stations at Woodvale, Ainsdale Beach and Birkdale Palace have also disappeared, this time beneath the road scheme that uses the old rail route through the dunes. Amidst this loss, it is all the more amazing that the portico and clock tower of the 1894 Lord Street station still survive. Following closure, in 1954 it became a bus depot, and was reported as little changed in the 1980s, except that the trackbed between the platforms had been filled in and there were buses amongst the roof pillars! The depot in turn closed in 1987, and the site was eventually used for a supermarket. This involved demolition of the station interior, but the frontage was preserved and restored to add to the fine array of buildings on Lord Street.

The Liverpool, Southport & Preston Junction Railway

As if one loss-making line to Southport wasn't enough, the WLR was also responsible for this project in 1884. Despite the grandiose title, all that resulted was a seven mile branch from the WLR at Meols Cop Junction, east of Southport, to the SCLER at Hillhouse Junction. The hope was that the Manchester, Sheffield & Lincolnshire Railway would take over the line (and the WLR), but this never materialised, nor did the hoped-for through workings from Blackburn to Liverpool. Instead the line remained an impoverished rural branch, with occasional specials, especially to Aintree on Grand National day.

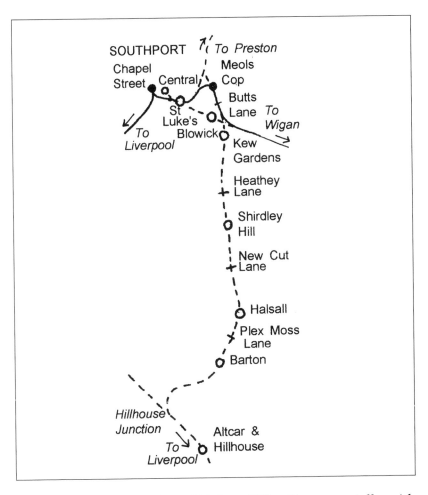

Construction started in 1884, but difficulties, especially with the five-span viaduct over the LYR at Blowick, delayed completion until 1887. Even then the opening day had to be postponed when the contractor, claiming non-payment of his fees, removed rails at both ends of the line! Initially there were six trains daily (three on Sundays), stopping at Meols Cop and Kew Gardens (named after a nearby park) within Southport, and the villages

125

of Shirdley Hill, Halsall and Barton, before terminating at Altcar & Hillhouse station. Here passengers could change onto trains on the SCLER, but they were few in number, and the railway went bankrupt two years after its opening.

In 1897, the line, now down to four trains a day, was taken over by the LYR. Nine years later it used one of its Kerr Stuart railmotors to start perhaps the most famous of these services, known locally as 'Altcar Bob'. Whether the name referred to the cost of a journey in the early days (one shilling), a driver, or just small engines generally, remains in doubt. Halts were added at New Cut Lane and Plex Moss Lane, and later at Butts Lane and Heathey Lane. No platforms or buildings were constructed at these halts, just a bed of cinders. Waiting for a train must have been an eerie experience after dark, when passengers had to hope that they would be spotted by the driver, often by striking matches!

Downholland (formerly Barton) station in its flat surroundings in 1949. This had been the terminus for 'Altcar Bob' from 1926 till the end of the service in 1939, and was still in use for goods services. (Stations UK)

The railmotor runs had increased to 16 return trips daily (nine on Sundays) by 1910, but already a majority of trains finished at Barton, rather than carrying on to a connection at Altcar & Hillhouse. The idea of a through passenger service ended in 1926 when all trains terminated at Barton, by then called Downholland. The line remained the epitome of a rural branch, with stories told about it for decades after. Tales of youngsters given unofficial turns at driving and firing, the guard left behind in the Blue Bell pub at Barton, trains stopped while the crew retrieved pheasants hit by the loco or even felled by a well-aimed lump of coal – these and many more have added to the legend of 'Altcar Bob'. However well-loved it may have been, improved roads and bus services in the 1930s steadily reduced usage until the LMS announced the end of passenger services. The last train was a conventional one, not a railmotor, on the final Saturday evening return from Southport on 24th September 1938.

The last activity on the line was track-lifting of the section to Shirdley Hill, kept in use until 1964 for storage of carriages from Southport. The work train is headed by BR class 02 D2851. (B.G. Barlow, courtesy J.A. Peden)

The surviving LS&PJR station – Meols Cop – with a Southport to Rochdale train in January 2003. (Author)

Less survives at the site of Shirdley Hill station – just a plaque beneath a street sign! (Author)

Freight lasted until July 1952, though down to a single 'Downholland goods' each weekday by the late 1940s. The tracks were left in place from Meols Cop to Shirdley Hill for another twelve years, for the storage of excursion rolling stock. Much of the line has disappeared beneath farmland, leaving only half a dozen road bridges and a few remnants of stations – platforms at Barton, steps at Plex Moss Lane halt, and a plaque at Shirdley Hill! The trackbed is more easily identifiable beyond Barton, where it has been used as a nature reserve, and on towards Hillhouse Junction. However, in one respect the LS&PJR has left more than most other 'lost' railways – one of its stations is still in use today. This is Meols Cop, where the closure of the LYR direct line in 1965 means that trains between Southport and Wigan still use the station and ¾ mile of the former LS&PJR route.

9
Towards The Mersey

*Blackburn to Chorley/Chorley to Wigan
(via Boar's Head)/Chorley to Wigan (via Hindley)/
Ormskirk-Rainford-St Helens*

*Ex-LYR 0-6-0 no 52194 hauls a goods train from the Blackburn line into
Chorley in September 1952. (F.W. Shuttleworth)*

Blackburn to Chorley

This was the outermost link in an ambitious scheme to connect
Blackburn, once the world's largest cotton-weaving town, to the
Mersey at Garston Dock, south of Liverpool. The St Helens
Canal & Railway Company had first built a line south to
Runcorn Gap (later Widnes) in 1832, and then extended west to

Garston 20 years later. The Lancashire Union Railway (LUR) was formed in 1864 to link these lines to Blackburn, via Wigan. It was backed by the LNWR but opposed by the LYR, so the outcome was a compromise whereby the LYR and the LUR would jointly build the Blackburn-Chorley section.

The 8½ mile line opened in 1869, climbing from the Blackburn-Preston line at Cherry Tree, 2 miles west of Blackburn, with two 80 ft high embankments and stations at Feniscowles and Withnell, before a summit of 600 ft at Brinscall station. Steam-hauled goods trains from Blackburn usually required the help of a banking engine for the 1 in 60 gradients up to Brinscall. Downhill to Chorley there was a further station at Heapey and a nine-arch viaduct 40 ft above the Leeds and Liverpool Canal.

Most passenger trains were local services to Chorley and Wigan, originally shared by the LNWR via Boar's Head, and the LYR through Hindley. By 1904 the service was operated by the LNWR only, with eleven stopping trains each way on weekdays

Withnell station building in 1998. All the line's stations were built in this style, except for Brinscall which was single-storey. (Author)

131

Unlikely candidates for a 'Strategic Reserve' at Heapey in 1960, with 0-6-0 no 51404, originally built by the LYR in 1883, rebuilt as a saddle tank twelve years later and finally withdrawn in 1959. (A.G. Ellis)

and four on Sundays. There were similar services into the 1950s (twelve and three trains respectively). Long-distance passenger traffic was generally confined to Wakes Weeks holiday trains, but in the late 19th century Blackburn to London through carriages were routed over the line, and in the 1920s and 1930s there was a daily train to North Wales. Freight was dominated by coal and cotton, but also included perishable fruit, especially bananas, en route from Garston Docks. The line was well provided with short industrial branches, to a cotton mill at Abbey Village, quarries at Withnell, and a bleachworks and War Department complex at Heapey. This latter site, now closed, has long been rumoured to be one of the locations for the 'Strategic Reserve' of steam locomotives supposedly hidden away in various parts of the country!

The line's closure was featured in the *Chorley Guardian* as 'End of the hikers' railway', referring to the use of Heapey station for walkers setting off to the nearby hills. Passenger services had ended in 1960, but freight kept the line open for a further six years, except for Cherry Tree to Feniscowles which was the last section to close in 1968. The Radnedge family moved into the station house at Feniscowles in 1956, and were thus there for the last years of passenger services. Alec Radnedge worked as the signalman at Feniscowles, and received a commendation for his prompt action in halting a passenger train at Brinscall, following a landslip into the adjacent Leeds and Liverpool Canal at Feniscowles. Traffic declined in later years, and was eventually down to a weekly goods train delivering pulp to Feniscowles' paper mills, though the line saw a rare visit by Britannia 70015 *Apollo* on a railtour in May 1967. The Radnedges stayed until

One of the last uses of steam on the line was this class 8F 2-8-0 sent with a crane to a derailment at Feniscowles, as seen from the signal box with the station building in the distance. (A. Radnedge)

The real 'Railway Children'? The Radnedges on the steam crane sent to the Feniscowles derailment in 1967. (A. Radnedge)

1974; by then the signal cabin had been burnt down (by British Railways), and the station area vandalised and plagued by thieves. The station was then demolished and replaced by the present-day 'Station House' bungalow.

Brinscall station – unusually for the line a single-storey build-ing – was also demolished, but Withnell and Heapey survive. Withnell station is actually at Abbey Village, and includes a miniature railway connecting the one-time platforms! The sta-tion building at Heapey has been much extended, and is used as a cattery and kennels. There is a walkable stretch of trackbed used as a nature reserve between Abbey Village and Brinscall, plus shorter lengths that can be walked through Chorley. The 'Three Arch Bridge' still crosses the A674 west of Blackburn, but the viaduct approaching Chorley was demolished in 1968, watched by a crowd of 2,000 people.

Chorley to Wigan (via Boar's Head)

After a break of three miles using the LYR line between Preston and Bolton through Chorley (opened 1841), the Blackburn to Garston Docks route resumed with a link to Boar's Head, 2½ miles north of Wigan on the West Coast Main Line. This four mile section was built by the LUR, opened in 1869 and was operated by the LNWR. Stations were provided at White Bear (named after a nearby pub) and Red Rock, as well as the junction station at Boar's Head, another pub location. The major construction feature was close to this junction where the line was carried across the Douglas valley on a viaduct of seven wrought-iron spans at a height of 86 ft above the river. There was a second crossing of the Douglas closer to Adlington, involving the three-arch Waterhouse viaduct. Nearby was the level crossing at Harrison Road, where the locking of the gates across the road at weekends once caused an understandable public outcry.

Passenger services were initially similar to those on the Blackburn to Chorley line, with eleven trains a day in 1904 heading towards Wigan (two on Sundays), although this link did see occasional Anglo-Scottish expresses when the main line north of Wigan was closed for engineering work. It was also much used for Wakes Weeks relief trains to London and South West England. Regular services had, however, declined by 1940, as more weekday trains used the LYR Blackrod to Hindley alternative just to the east, and no Sunday services ran on this line to Boar's Head. Closures began in 1949, with both Boar's Head and Red Rock stations closing to passengers. White Bear station lasted until 1960 when the line closed to regular passenger

A long-term resident on the Boar's Head line, LYR 0-6-0 goods engine no 1300, is here seen at Carnforth in the 1980s after restoration to full working order. (Author's collection)

services, which had been known in earlier years as 'Chorley Bob'. Freight continued but diminished when the line was sin-gled in the mid 1960s, final closure coming on 25th May 1971. One interesting relic during these last years was LYR loco no 1300, built at Horwich in 1896, which spent the period 1961–76 on display in the former goods yard at White Bear, then owned by Faircloughs (now Amec's White Bear Yard). This loco is now at the East Lancashire Railway (see Chapter 7), where it was operational from 1995–9 as British Railways no 52322.

Little is now left of this line. Both viaducts were demolished, Waterhouse viaduct by 12 year old Jacob Browne! He had won the Adlington Community Association raffle to detonate the charges on April 23rd 1983. Nothing is left of Boar's Head sta-tion, although the former booking office at White Bear survives. Red Rock retains 'The Old Railway Station', though much

White Bear station seen shortly before the arrival of the last scheduled passenger train on 2nd January 1960. (K. Hick collection)

Roughly the same scene in 2002 with only the former booking office left from the station, then in use as a café for the marina on the nearby Leeds & Liverpool Canal. (Author)

137

rebuilt, with almost two miles of walkable trackbed north towards Adlington. As the route is designated for cyclists and horse-riders it can be very muddy for walkers.

Chorley to Wigan (via Hindley)

The LYR branch used for this service was a classic example of Victorian duplication of routes. The LYR opposed the LNWR-backed LUR scheme to link Blackburn and Wigan. A compromise was reached whereby the LUR and the LYR would share the Blackburn to Chorley section, but each company would build its own link onwards to Wigan. Like the LUR line, this LYR link left the Preston to Bolton line, but at Red Moss Junction near Blackrod, and ran for 3¼ miles to Crow Nest Junction on the Bolton to Wigan line of 1848. The branch opened in 1868, and two stations were built at Hilton House and Dicconson Lane & Aspull. Both, temporarily closed between 1917 and 1919, were reduced to halts in 1945 and 1936 respectively, and closed finally in 1954. They had been used by the LYR's Chorley to Wigan service, which in 1904 amounted to ten trains each way on weekdays and three on Sundays. In the 1950s services were down to seven weekday trains, but five of these had started at Blackburn. By then the only Sunday services between Blackburn and Wigan were the three trains on this line, as there were no trains on the alternative route to the west. However, local services on both lines ended in January 1960.

That would have been the end for the branch but for a new role that it had taken on in the 1880s. In 1888 the LYR opened a direct route from Salford to Wigan, bypassing Bolton, and the following year linked this to the Blackrod to Hindley line by a spur from Dobbs Brow Junction. The formerly minor branch could then be used by expresses from Manchester to Blackpool, Edinburgh and Glasgow. Prominent among these were the Blackpool residential expresses – see Chapter 3. The last expresses on the line ran in September 1968, after which it went out of use. Traces of the route can still be seen in places, but nothing remains at either station site.

Ex-LYR 4-6-0 no 10448 in action in August 1947, on the Blackpool residential express service that regularly used the Blackrod-Hindley line. (F. Dean)

In January 2003, a modern replacement for the Blackpool service has just passed the former Red Moss Junction, where the route to Hindley used to fork right. (Author)

Ormskirk-Rainford-St Helens

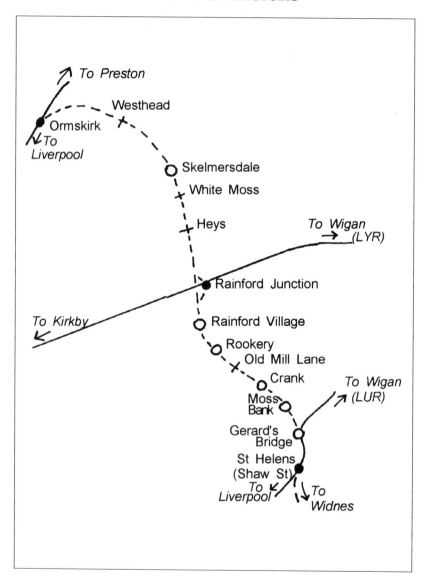

Much further west, the St Helens Railway was also linked to Ormskirk, a market town on the West Lancashire Plain, now popular as a residential outlier of Merseyside. Ormskirk's first rail connection was the Liverpool, Ormskirk & Preston Railway, part of the ELR by the time of its opening in 1849. The Act for this line had included a branch from Ormskirk to Skelmersdale, and work began on this in 1847, but was suspended the following year. It was not resumed until 1857, this time with an extension to meet the St Helens Railway at Rainford Junction station (Rainford since 1973) on the 1848 line linking Manchester Victoria to Liverpool Exchange. Both sections were completed by 1858. The initial passenger services were worked separately by the two companies, meeting at Rainford Junction! This pattern was continued by the successor companies, the LYR in the case of the ELR, and the LNWR absorbing the St Helens Railway. Even in the last year (1951) of passenger working over the whole line, most services ran separately from Ormskirk and St Helens to Rainford Junction, despite a through single track bypassing the junction and mostly used by freight trains.

Taking the northern half first, the only intermediate station between Ormskirk and Rainford Junction was Skelmersdale (called Blaguegate after the nearby colliery until 1874), although halts were added at Westhead, White Moss and Heys in 1906. This was for the introduction of a railmotor service by the LYR, providing 19 return trips on weekdays and eleven on Sundays. Services stayed popular in the 1920s and 30s, with jazz music evenings in Skelmersdale leading to the nickname 'Skem Jazzer' as an alternative to 'Skem Dodger' for the trains. In the 1930s the railmotors were replaced by push-pull locos with conventional coaches, but usage dropped away after 1945, and in 1951 the halts closed. Passenger services to Skelmersdale and Rainford Junction survived until 1956. Goods services south and north of Skelmersdale lasted another five and seven years respectively, with the line closing altogether in 1964.

At Rainford Junction, the LYR provided a fine set of stone buildings for the northern side, but to the south the LNWR could only manage a pair of wooden huts. LNWR passenger

141

Ormskirk station looking south in 1958 with an electric train from Liverpool. (R. Stephens)

The much reduced station at Ormskirk in 2002. A little-used single track for Preston continues into the distance, but there is no sign of the former curve to the right for Rainford. (Author)

A worm's eye view of Skelmersdale station in 1964, the year this section of line closed completely. (J.A. Peden)

trains were also less frequent, with eight trains to St Helens on weekdays and three on Sundays in 1906. Other stations were built, usually with distinctive wooden shelters, at Rainford Village, Rookery, Crank, Moss Bank and Gerard's Bridge. The latter closed in 1904, and in 1911 the LNWR introduced a short-lived railmotor service from St Helens to Rainford Junction, with an additional halt at Old Mill Lane. Crank too became a halt in 1940, but local passenger services, known locally as the 'Flying Flea', ended as early as 1951. Diversions, passenger excursions and goods traffic, including through freight trains, continued to use the line for another thirteen years, when it was cut back to Pilkington's Sidings south of Rainford.

The line was further shortened at the St Helens end in 1967, and now only about 2 miles still have track. A mile of this is in use for passenger trains from Wigan to St Helens, coming off the line opened by the LUR in 1869 as part of the Blackburn to

143

Rookery station in 1957, six years after closure to passengers. Note the distinctive style of the wooden shelter as provided for all the stations on this ex-LNWR section of the line. (J.A. Peden)

Garston Docks route dealt with earlier in this chapter. A short stretch either side of the East Lancs Road (A580) has been used for a road, and the line has largely disappeared from there to Rainford, although railway cottages at Crank and the station house at Rookery remain. The route through the village of Rainford has been used as a linear park, and Rainford station survives (though no longer 'Junction') with services from Wigan to Kirkby. Almost nothing is left of the Rainford to Ormskirk section, even the Railway pub at Skelmersdale is now the Roundabout!

10
Railway Town

Blackrod to Horwich and 'Horwich Fork'

In 1884, the LYR was actively searching for a new site to replace its works at Miles Platting. Various locations had been suggested, including one at Great Harwood (Chapter 6), but by the time the directors met on May 21st, none had been accepted. At the meeting, the company's surveyor and land agent, Elias Dorning, referred to that morning's paper, in which there was notice of an auction of 650 acres of land at Horwich, west of Bolton. This was a new possibility, which was investigated, approved, and successfully bid for, all within the next six days. Thus the LYR came to Horwich, for an initial outlay of £36,000 at the auction.

Although the site itself could be described as 'greenfield', Horwich was not brought into existence by the railway company. The 1881 census showed a population of 3,761, with employment in cotton-manufacturing, farming, quarrying and brick-making. The LYR itself had provided a rail link to the former Bolton & Preston Railway at Horwich Road (the present-day Blackrod station). This was the 1¼ mile Horwich branch, opened in 1868 for goods and two years later for passenger services, but only to and from the direction of Preston.

The new works took in its first engines for repair in 1886, but was only really developed under J.A.F. Aspinall, appointed Chief Mechanical Engineer of the LYR in the October of that year. Three years later the first of 1,830 steam locomotives to be built at Horwich was completed. The last of these was in 1957, but loco production continued with diesel shunters for another five years. The rundown of facilities continued with the end of engine repair in 1964, by which time over 50,000 locos had been dealt with at the works. Carriage and wagon repair continued, and £400,000 was spent on providing facilities for the overhaul

'Wren', seen here at Horwich in 1953, is the only survivor of the works' 18 inch gauge 0-4-0ST locos. It is now preserved at the National Railway Museum, York. (B. Hilton)

of electric units in 1979, so that it was surprising that final closure (apart from the foundry) came in 1983. As well as 12½ miles of standard gauge track leading from the Horwich branch, the works had over 7 miles of 18 inch narrow gauge track, worked by diminutive 0-4-0 saddle tanks.

By the 1890s, Horwich Works employed 5,000 men and boys, and in the 1891 census the town's population had risen to 12,850. Rail access to the town (and works) had been improved in 1887 by the addition of a spur facing Bolton, known as 'Horwich Fork'. This allowed services from the town to Bolton and Manchester, and soon 20 trains a day were leaving the single platform. Various schemes were put forward to extend the station's rudimentary facilities, but all foundered on the problem of the narrow access under the nearby Chorley New Road.

The town's railway service was soon affected by trams and later buses, although some trains remained busy, notably the

146

The 'Blackrod Jerk' had been replaced by more conventional stock in this 1962 scene with BR Standard class 2MT no 84013 standing at Blackrod station with a Horwich service. (H.C. Casserley)

8.15 am departure for Bolton and Manchester. Local services for much of the day, however, were reduced to a shuttle to and from Blackrod. In LYR days this was often worked by new or repaired engines on trials. Later it became the preserve of one of the last ex-LYR railmotors in service. This was known locally as the 'Blackrod Jerk' and lasted until 1943, although its gas-lit coach stayed in use for another six years. Latterly almost all passengers to Horwich were employees at the works, and it was no surprise when closure, first proposed in 1961, came about in 1965. The last train was the 12.05 pm to Bolton on Saturday, 25th September, when loco no 42626 hauled two carriages packed with enthusiasts out of the station. Goods traffic continued for a few months more, finishing in April 1966. The Fork spur was removed the next year, but the original branch from Blackrod remained in use until the closure of the works.

The huge works, now used for the Horwich Loco Industrial Estate, still dominate the town with its streets named after

Ex-LMS class 4F 0-6-0 no 44501 on a railtour at Horwich station in September 1963, two years before closure. (G.W. Sharpe)

The station site is now Old Station Park, with only a set of loco wheels to commemorate the railway connection! (Author)

famous engineers (Stephenson, Brunel etc), but most other rail-way-influenced buildings, notably the Mechanics' Institute of 1888, have gone. Almost all trace of the railway itself has also disappeared, leaving only the Old Station Park to commemorate its site within the town.

Conclusion

So what has the county lost? Many places have merely seen a reduction in rail services. For example, Morecambe still has trains to Lancaster and Leeds, despite the loss of Promenade station (and the ex-LNWR Euston Road station) and the direct link to Lancaster via Scale Hall. However, such services are a shadow of past ones, with long-distance and excursion traffic now almost non-existent. In addition, surviving rail links often hide the extent of the losses. Southport, for instance, may still have two lines and five stations within its boundaries, but these are reduced from five and seventeen respectively a century ago. Nevertheless the reductions have still left these coastal towns, plus inland ones as varied as Ormskirk, Accrington, Clitheroe and Chorley, and the cities of Preston and Lancaster, with continuing rail links.

It is the places now without any rail connection that have suffered most. These range from villages such as Knott End, Glasson and Holcombe Brook to sizeable towns like Padiham, Longridge and especially Fleetwood. These have also seen their respective industries of textiles, quarrying and fishing decline with the railways that once served them. It is perhaps the former cotton towns that been hardest hit; for example, the isolated town of Bacup is now 9 miles from any working railway station. Yet descriptions from the 1930s depict its station as a bustling place, with people changing trains between its two lines, and shoppers and visitors arriving, along with businessmen for the local mills. Engines from the town's loco shed would be busy shunting carriages, and at work in the goods yard. Now all this has gone completely, leaving not a trace within the town.

To the local inhabitants, it was perhaps the links to the seaside, especially to Blackpool, that were most missed. For most, this was connected with the town's Wakes Week holiday, when, for days before, the local station's carriage sidings would fill

150

with coaches ready for the annual exodus on the long-awaited Saturday. For some, especially youngsters, trips to Blackpool were a more frequent event, as many towns saw regular Saturday specials. Horwich in the 1930s, for example, had a 5.30 pm departure at 2s 6d return, including admission to the dances at the Tower Ballroom or Winter Gardens. Such Blackpool specials were a feature of the rail services from places as far away as Whitworth at the eastern margins of Lancashire – a round trip of over 100 miles.

That brings us back to Blackpool, surely the scene of the greatest railway loss in the county. Yes, there are still rail services from North and South stations, but gone is Central station with its 14 platforms. Almost 40 years after the site was sold for 'redevelopment', what has this amounted to but car parks, access roads and empty land? This pattern is repeated throughout the county, with the vacated railway land rarely used for anything but a road scheme or a length of footpath. More often than not it has been taken over piecemeal for housing, garden extensions, warehousing and factory car parks, or just left empty. It is as if the rail closure has been part of a general shutdown of industry and trade within the area, with little brought in to replace it. At least while memories like those in this book can be collected, the railways and the society they served can still be commemorated.

Opening and Final Closure Dates of Lines to Regular Passenger Traffic

Line	Opened	Final Closure
Preston/Longridge	1.5.1840	2.6.1930
Poulton/Fleetwood	15.7.1840	1.6.1970
Lancaster/Morecambe (ex-Midland line)	12.6.1848	3.1.1966
Stubbins/Accrington	17.8.1848	5.12.1966
Skipton/Colne	2.10.1848	1.2.1970
Wennington/Lancaster	17.11.1849	3.1.1966
Clitheroe/Chatburn	22.6.1850	10. 9.1962
Bamber Bridge/Preston (ELR)	2.9.1850	7.10.1968
Bury/Bacup	1.10.1852*	5.12.1966°
St Helens/Rainford	1.2.1858	18.6.1951
Ormskirk/Rainford	1.3.1858	5.11.1956
Blackpool South/Blackpool Central	6.4.1863	2.11.1964
Blackrod/Hindley	14. 9.1868	4.1.1960¢
Blackburn/Chorley/Wigan (via Boar's Head)	1.12.1869	4.1.1960
Blackrod/Horwich	14. 2.1870	27.9.1965
Garstang & Catterall/Pilling	5.12.1870	31.3.1930
Earby/Barnoldswick	8. 2.1871	27.9.1965
Great Harwood Loop	15.10.1877*	2.12.1957
Chatburn/Hellifield	1.6.1880*	10.9.1962
Rochdale/Bacup	1.12.1881*	16.6.1947

Southport/Preston	6.9.1882*	7.9.1964
Bury/Holcombe Brook	6.11.1882	5.5.1952
Lancaster/Glasson Dock	9.7.1883	7.7.1930
Southport/Aintree	1.9.1884	7.1.1952
Southport/Hillhouse Jct (LS&PJR)	1.11.1887	26.9.1938
Grimsargh/Whittingham Hospital	June 1889	30.6.1957
Kirkham/Blackpool South		
('New Line')	30.5.1903	6.9.1965
Pilling/Knott End	30.8.1908	31.3.1930

Not included: 'Horwich Fork' 1887–1965, Poulton Curve 1899–1970

Note: Closure dates are those posted by the operating company, usually a Monday, with the last train on the previous Saturday/ Sunday (except Whittingham Hospital).

* Opened in stages up to this date
° Bury/Ramsbottom/Rawtenstall reopened as the East Lancashire Railway
¢ In use to Dobbs Brow Jct until 9.9.1968

Bibliography

Many of the following are out of print, but can still be obtained second-hand or consulted in libraries.

Bairstow, M. *Railways in East Lancashire* (Martin Bairstow)
Bairstow, M. *Railways of Blackpool and the Fylde* (Martin Bairstow)
Bairstow, M. *The East Lancashire Railway* (Martin Bairstow)
Bairstow, M. *The 'Little' North Western Railway* (Martin Bairstow)
Biddle, G. *Railways around Preston* (Foxline Publishing)
Binns, D. *Midland Lines Around Morecambe, Heysham and Lancaster* (Trackside Publications)
Binns, D. *The Skipton-Colne Railway and the Barnoldswick Branch* (Trackside Publications)
Catterall, J.E. *The West Lancashire Railway* (The Oakwood Press)
Holt, G.O. *A Regional History of the Railways of Great Britain: Volume 10: The North West* (David & Charles)
Joby, R.S. *Southport & Cheshire Lines Extension Railway* (Klofron Norwich)
McLoughlin, B. *Railway Heritage: Blackpool and the Fylde* (Silver Link Publishing)
Marshall, J. *Forgotten Railways: North West England* (David & Charles)
Nuttall, K. & Rawlings, T. *Railways Around Lancaster* (Dalesman Books)
Parker, N. *The Preston & Longridge Railway* (The Oakwood Press)
Rush, R.W. *The East Lancashire Railway* (The Oakwood Press)
Rush, R.W. & Price, M.R.C. *The Garstang & Knott End Railway* (The Oakwood Press)
Westall, K. D. *The Holcombe Brook Branch* (The Lancashire & Yorkshire Railway Society)

Westall, K.D. *The North Lancs Loop* (The Lancashire & Yorkshire Railway Society)

Wilby, C.R. *Railways Around East Lancashire* (Wyvern Publications)

Wray, T. *The Bacup Branch: Ramsbottom-Stubbins-Rawtenstall* (The Lancashire & Yorkshire Railway Society)

Wray, T. *The Bacup Branch: Rochdale-Facit-Bacup* (The Lancashire & Yorkshire Railway Society)

Index